THE SUN IN MAN

SECRETS OF THE ROYAL ART

JOHNNY MANNAZ

The Sun in Man:
Secrets of the Royal Art

Johnny Mannaz
Copyright © 2022

Cover design by Srdjan Vidakovic
Book design by www.delaney-designs.com

All rights reserved. No part of this book may be used or reproduced by any means, graphic, electronic, or mechanical, including photocopying, recording, taping or by any information storage retrieval system without the written permission of the author except in the case of brief quotations in critical articles and reviews.

ISBN Softcover: 978-1-7345713-3-2
ISBN Hardcover: 978-1-7345713-5-6
ISBN Ebook: 978-1-7345713-1-8

1.) Spirituality-Solar, 2.) Philosophy-Men, 3.) Self-Actualization (Psychology) 4.) Mythology- Psychological Aspects, 5.) Magic 6.) Occultism 7.) Thelema

First edition published in 2022 by Johnny Mannaz and Mannaz Enterprises, under the Mannaz Media imprint.

LIVE YOUR WILL@www.thekingscurriculum.com

Dedicated to:

"The Anthropocosmos"

"Arise, ye who are a Sun of great light…
Great Spirit of the Sun-Born,
Shine through the shadow of the flesh,
Be free of the bonds of darkness.

Make your Spirit as a torch,
So that even in darkness,
Thine own light pours forth.

Be thou a Sovereign:
One who becomes one with the light."

-altered and paraphrased from
Thoth's Emerald Tablet

TABLE OF CONTENTS

Introduction: Man the Pentagram – *The Order of Earth* 23

Chapter One: The Daimon – *The Sun Within* 31

Chapter Two: True Will – *The Father of Creation* 69

Chapter Three: The Holy Grail – *The Mother of Deeds* 93

Chapter Four: The Sword – *Guardian of Right Action* 111

Chapter Five: The Pantacle Coin – *Art as the birth of Reality* 133

Chapter Six: God's Plan, the Hexagram – *The Order of Heaven* 161

Epilogue: *Closing the Circle* 173

Circumambulation 176

This book as a Pantacle 177

Etymological foundations of chapter concepts 179

THE SUN IN MAN:

Secrets of the Royal Art

*"Only that day dawns to which we are awake.
There is more day to dawn.
The Sun is but a morning star."*

- Henry David Thoreau, Walden

SECRETS OF THE ROYAL ART

WHAT IS THE ROYAL ART?

The ROYAL ART is dedicated to the original, secret, sublime system of Spiritual Sovereignty that once ruled the ancient world.

It embodies the royal practice of wisdom as a SPIRITUAL TECHNOLOGY.

This Spiritual Technology was first handed down as a divine inheritance, given to Man for the purposes of building a sacred order on Earth, one to reflect the order of the Heavens.

In possession of this ART, the Individual takes creative command of their existence, putting both their growth and well-being in their own hands.

The goal of the ROYAL ART is the satisfaction of ALL ORDERS of an Individual's being. Essential to this is the understanding that the satisfaction of ALL ORDERS of the Individual's being is not possible if elements of either the higher or lower orders of their being are lacking.

Here the ancient adage "As above, so below" represents an interdependence and cooperation of those different orders. The ART represents the ability to transfer energy from the lower order to the higher order and visa versa.

In this respect, command of the higher order confers command of the lower order.

Thus, The ROYAL ART is the technique of attaining Man's highest, most valued ends, *in the most efficient means possible.*

The ROYAL ART represents that elemental wisdom essential to the endeavors of *Creation*.

This is a craft, an art, and a power.

In this craft, the Individual causes changes to occur, in their internal world, in such a way that it provokes the external world to respond to that change in kind. Thus, it is the art of magnifying and directing one's heightened, subjective state, via their WILL, into a medium capable of manifesting its resemblance in the objective world.

This requires synchronizing subjective reality with objective existence, aligning the two as ONE. To achieve this, the Individual unites their own TRUE WILL with *the plan of the whole.*

For the Individual, now creator, these are the components of taking up command or rulership of their consciousness and assuming sovereign authorship of life.

In the early stages of learning their craft, artists typically master what are called the "tools of their art."

The tools of the SOVEREIGN SYSTEM are both simple, in essence, and profoundly deep in implication.

These ritual objects are external representations of internal processes. As simple components, they form an interrelated family of ideas whose interdependent relationships provide the underlying structure to the entire system.

Here they are represented in symbolic form, as simple objects with profound meanings.

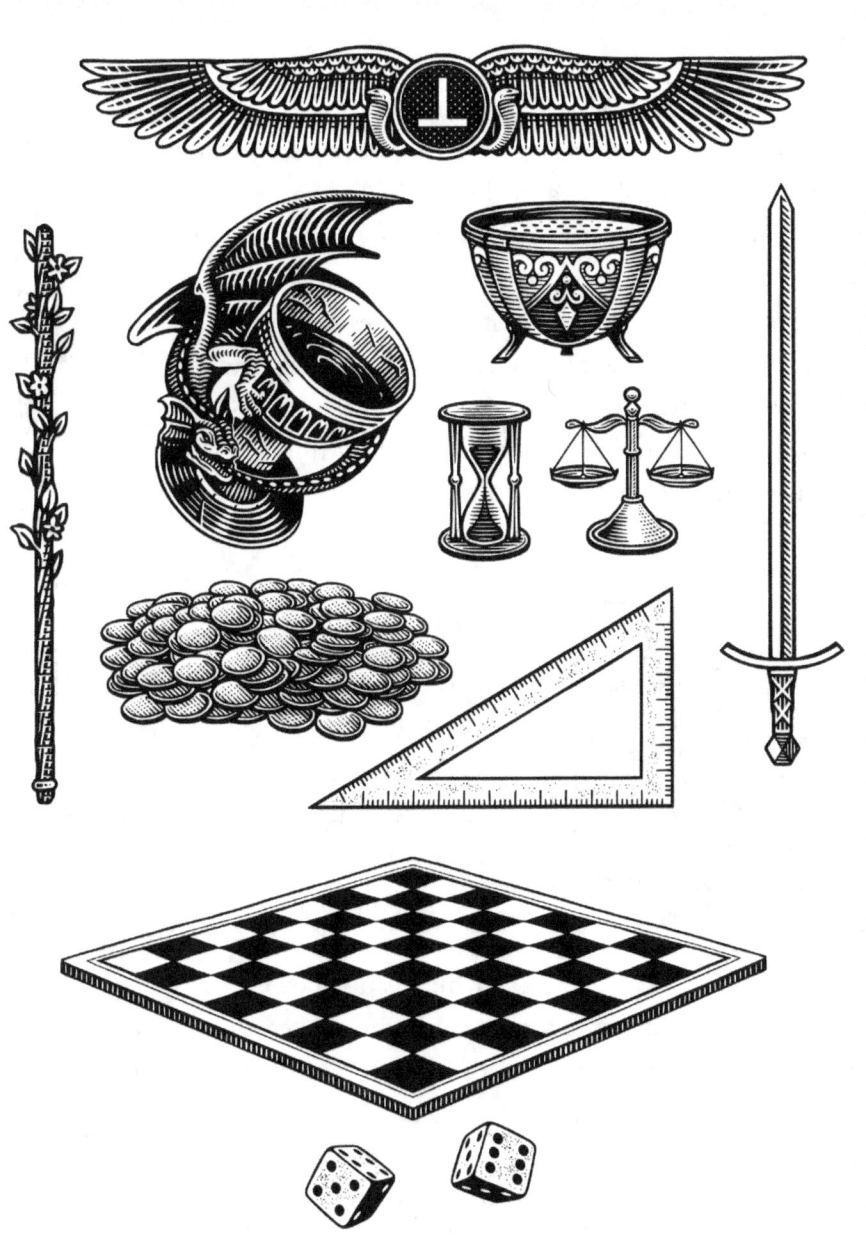

"One the Art, One the Material, One the Crucible."
— Old Medieval Tradition

The Rod:

Imagine the Rod as a budding branch from the Tree of Life.

This branch represents both your connection to the greater processes of life and the original, organic driver of your consciousness. The energy it activates is the primal libido of your innermost nature.

Symbolically, this branch embodies the Individual's TRUE WILL, the active aspect of one's being, the essential element that drives one toward their aspirations. It is the divine force desiring to fulfill itself by fulfilling all the needs embedded in one's nature.

The Cup:

Imagine this Cup as a divine Chalice, also known as the HOLY GRAIL.

This Cup represents silent meditation, during which the mind becomes a vessel open to receiving. By its shape it indicates that it is open only to "that which is up above."

It collects higher energies and transmutes them into gnosis, or understanding. The nature of the Cup is reception and reflection, most often achieved through states of contemplation.

Symbolically, this Cup embodies the power of UNDERSTANDING. This understanding is the reward of EXPERIENCE and results from the mind's unconscious synthesis of collected energies as integrated awareness, resulting in: moments of illumination, a deepening of intuition, and an awareness of the profound mysteries of synchronicity.

The Sword:

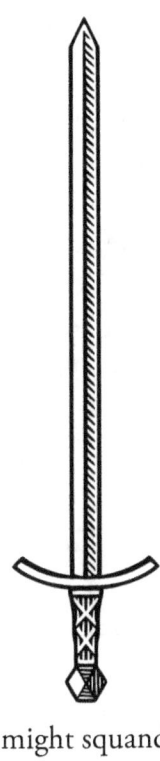

In hierarchical descent, imagine this Sword as a dutiful son faithfully serving the WILL of its Father.

Guided by WILL, this razor-sharp cutting instrument represents analysis, the intellectual faculty that adopts actions to ends. The powers of the Sword are the qualities of intellect which serve to demarcate boundaries and limits, recognize distinctions and command the ability to reason objectively. The Sword is a weapon of discernment and decision, one we need to make hard choices with enough boldness to face their inevitable consequences.

Symbolically, the Sword embodies the powers of REASON. It is not only razor sharp but lighting fast and able to move in any direction on command. Its point is aimed at efficiency. The Sword guides our actions by cutting away threads of unnecessary entanglements that might squander the energy of our WILL. It can be used to cleave problems, cutting them down to more manageable parts.

The Pantacle Coins:

Imagine the Coins as the life of Earth and all its fruits. Principally, they are the manifest current of all tangible things, the swirling material of physical existence, endlessly changing hands and changing shape. It is the material we build with, including our physical body.

The Coins represent the practical principle of spiritual power. They are both the material we work with and the medium we work through in this life. Their circulation is the interplay of events and circumstances, both their causes and effects. Managing this power requires a good deal of "common sense," which means a grounded knowledge of what is and what is not materially possible.

Symbolically, the Coins embody the nature of gold and currency. Developing this element is the science of economics, the art of tracing consequences and recognizing inevitable implications. Properly applied it represents determined action and purposeful behavior directed toward a given END.

Strategy is the ART of forming circumstances to increase one's wealth of positive experiences. The Coin brings to mind the need for prudence, mindfully tending to our business, carefully considering our choice of investments, which also means making appropriate sacrifices – setting aside some goals in favor of others. Mastering this power means comprehending both general and secondary consequences as we trace the effects of our actions from the short run to the long run.

It is through an astute attention to fluctuations, of both increase and decrease, that we cultivate this force. Mastery of the Coin means the careful calculation of probabilities as well as the ability to accurately estimate **VALUE**.

The Censor:

Imagine the Censor as the world of the ethereal current that lies between ideas and reality. It's on this plane that manifest things begin to take on a recognizable outline.

The Censor represents the power of one's creative imagination, that invocative medium through which potential creations are shaped. Like wispy clouds of smoke that take on a momentary form, this dream world is where one is free to envision the future they wish to create without being burdened by its necessary details. It is in this world that things can be seen that are not yet real. It is exceedingly important, here, to be able to distinguish between those things we dream that have the potential to become real (under the proper circumstances) and those which could probably never become real because their designs are just too ungrounded.

Symbolically, the incense smoke that arises from the Censor is the dream world whose imagery and inspirations desire to poke through the unconscious veil of the Mind and make their presence known. We all experience states of imagination. We enter and exit these dreamlike trances, both by day and night. They are those moments in which we're taken away to faroff, internal worlds both alluring and frightful. It is the mental state where our deepest fears and highest hopes can be experienced without ever even being materially manifest. This mental world is the drafting table, not only of madmen, but of artists, builders, geniuses and prophets.

The Dice:

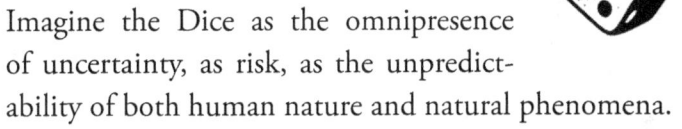

Imagine the Dice as the omnipresence of uncertainty, as risk, as the unpredictability of both human nature and natural phenomena.

The Dice represent the fundamental implication that this world is full of uncertainty, the ever-present possibility of error in action, the inability to predict the future course of the world with precision.

Symbolically, the Dice embody the power of chance, the hand of fate and the wheel of fortune. Because the influence of these factors cannot be accurately estimated in our calculations they represent an eternal truth – that a certain amount of risk and uncertainty cannot be eliminated from our plans.

The Scales:

Imagine the Scales as the ongoing dynamic of Yin and Yang, the inherent force of equilibrium, nature's continual desire to rectify gross imbalances, as well as the weighing and measuring of things of value. It is the instrument that distinguishes brass from gold.

The Scales represent considerations of exchange and trade including the economy of mental and physical states. All of life goes through phases of ebbing and flowing, waxing and waning. How do we make the most use of life's natural fluctuations of energies, in currents and currency, in value and values?

Symbolically, the scales also embody the power of objective judgements, the weighing out of important considerations. If we are to build a wealth of worthwhile experiences in life then we must take into consideration the exchanges we make along the way. Implied in the scales is also the notion of justice, or developing the objective faculty of good judgment. Here our attention is brought to the ancient Egyptian conception of Maat. What will the poor exchanges and choices we make today cost us tomorrow? How can we increase our wealth and energies without upsetting the balance of life?

The Hour glass:

Imagine the Hour-glass as time, the all-pervading limitations of life as well as the force that naturally brings things, through processes, to their completion.

The Hour-glass represents the fundamental principle of scarcity. In choosing to satisfy certain ends there are others which must go unsatisfied. All of life takes place under the constraints of time. Man's physical life is not immortal, our time on Earth is limited.

Symbolically, the Hour-glass embodies the powers of time as the means life uses to arrive at its ends. The necessity imposed on life by the limits of time highlight the need for choice. We must choose among ends, determined not only by the resources available to us but also accounting for the time allotted to attain those ends.

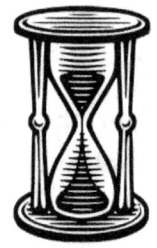

The Board:

Imagine the Board as the landscape of human interaction, the features that indicate various opportunities and threats, the quality of your plans and move choices that may possibly increase your position and aims in the game of life.

The Board represents the need to evaluate certain positions depending on circumstances that make a move more or less valuable. Like chess, the game of life moves through three distinct phases: the opening, the middle game, and the end game. These reflect the three stages of life. The opening includes our childhood through to our early adulthood. These are our "first moves," a time when we begin a logical development of our "pieces."

The middle game represents our transition into middle life, characterized by increased complexity and an ongoing struggle for positional and material advantage. If the game (life) lasts long enough, play then transitions into the endgame, which is characterized by attempts to deliver checkmate, i.e. lasting positional advantage and the attainment of long desired ends (ultimate life goals/legacy).

Symbolically, the Board embodies the powers of long-term strategic thinking, a mastery of tempo as a description of time measured in *advantageous moves*. Tempo speaks of the number of moves it takes to accomplish something efficiently. With each wasted move, our opponent (time) gains an advantage. We want to avoid losing momentum by making every move count toward our ultimate goal.

"The Call of the Lord"

The central branch of this system is the budding life of WILL.

Most people already know of "Willpower," which is their ability to cause something to occur (effects through actions) by *force of their will*. Studies show that a lack of willpower is the primary reported reason that Individuals fail in their undertakings in life.

TRUE WILL is a term that partakes of the common notion of willpower, yet transcends that ideal with a definition that is closer in association to "a calling," or manifestation of the Individual's authentic essence. TRUE WILL is the force behind what a person wants to BECOME in this life.

It could be said that TRUE WILL is the ACT of satisfying the deepest needs of consciousness. It embodies the ultimate endeavor toward which the Individual feels an obligation to succeed. In this sense TRUE WILL represents the "requirements" of consciousness that lead to Individual wholeness, a process which psychologist Carl Jung called INDIVIDUATION.

The greatest attainment of human life, in Jung's opinion, is the attainment of WHOLENESS. That's to say the fulfillment of the Individual's essential drive, the essence of all the needs embedded in their nature.

TRUE WILL represents the growth and development toward "higher needs," what American psychologist Abraham Maslow termed "Self-Actualization."

Maslow, best known for creating *Maslow's hierarchy of needs* developed the theory that psychological health is predicated on fulfilling a pyramid of innate human needs, beginning with physiological needs such as: food, water, warmth and rest, and once fulfilled ascends through a hierarchy of other needs including security and safety, social needs such as intimate relationships and a sense of belonging, esteem needs such as prestige and feelings of accomplishment.

Each time a level of human needs are met, the focus moves to still higher levels all the way up to what Maslow called SELF-ACTUALIZATION.

Building this pyramid of self-actualization represents *the supreme creative act*.

TRUE WILL represents the Individual's own path of fulfilling this entire pyramid of needs, from the most basic lower orders all the way up to the capstone of completion – SELF-ACTUALIZATION. An imperfect or incomplete satisfaction of this "pyramid of needs" would mean a stunted expression of the Individual's essential nature.

Failure to attain this possibility of ultimate fulfillment means a failure to harvest the full potential of SELF.

Thus, the attainment of SELF-ACTUALIZATION, or complete fulfillment, is the most important of human endeavors. This means the fulfillment of the *highest orders of one's being*.

Attaining the pyramid's capstone is the very reason for ensuring the solid foundation of all the previous lower orders of material concerns. Basic survival is just a base for building higher aspirations.

As TRUE WILL embodies the fulfillment of all the requirements of consciousness that lead to the experience of wholeness, inherent in this WILL is the desire to command the manifestation of things upon which this satisfaction depends, including love, wealth, health, and the conscious fulfillment of a life's purpose.

Some of the essential qualities of this drive are ENERGY, INITIATIVE, CONCENTRATION, DETERMINATION, AND PERSISTENCE.

At its heart, the Individual who realizes their TRUE WILL discovers their divine purpose, the very reason for their being, and exalts that purpose with an act of concentrated WILL, one which unifies their being and *directs their expression of life-energy*.

The activation of this 'life-energy' represents the Individual's contact with the life-energy of UNIVERSAL WILL whose expression lives through the Individual as a CALLING. *This is the Call of the Lord.*

From here it is just one small step to say that, for the Individual, connecting with the current of their own TRUE WILL is also an expression of UNIVERSAL WILL, as it relates to themselves. In this way, their WILL becomes sacred.

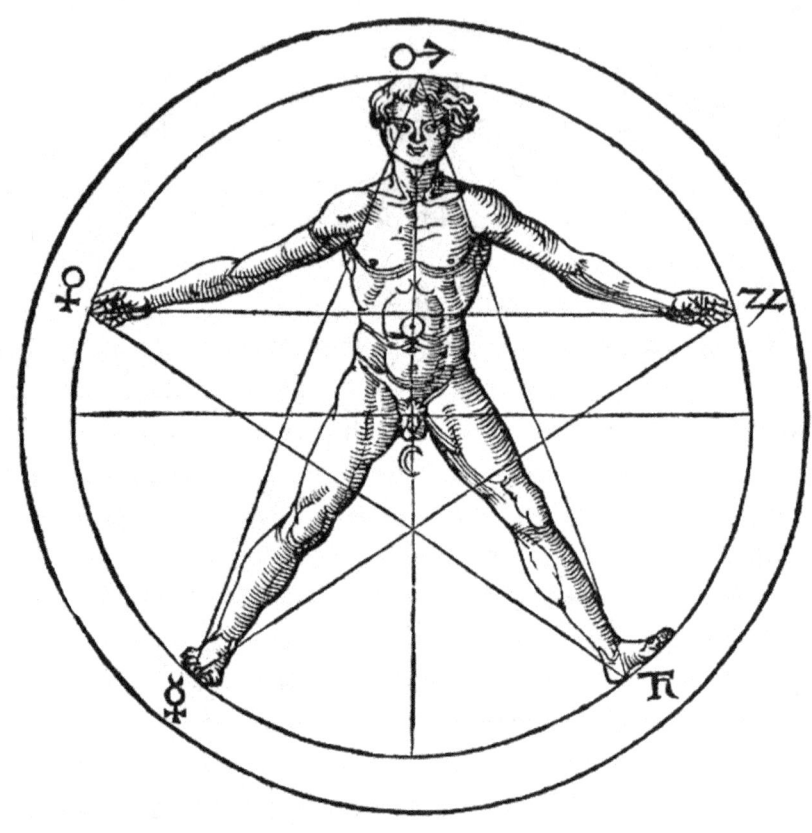

From Heinrich Cornelius Agrippa's Three Books of Occult Philosophy

INTRODUCTION

MAN THE PENTAGRAM:
The Order of Earth

The Pentagram: "Symbolic of Man, health and love, and of the quintessence acting upon matter. The Pentagram comprises the four limbs of the body plus the head which controls them, and likewise the four fingers plus the thumb and the four cardinal points together with the center. The hieros gamos is signified by the number five, since it represents the union of the principle of heaven (three) with that of the Magna Mater (two). Geometrically, it is the pentagram, or the five-pointed star. It corresponds to pentagonal symmetry, a common characteristic of organic nature, to the golden section (noted by Pythagoreans) and to the five senses representing the five 'forms' of matter."

- A Dictionary of Symbols, J.E. Cirlot

A Pentagram, is a five-pointed star, often within a circle. It's one of the oldest markings known to humankind.

Commonly, the five points of the Pentagram are said to represent the elements: earth, sky, fire, water, with Spirit representing the top most point.

Its origins date back to 8,000 years with the earliest examples found as petroglyphs in the Alpine region of Europe.

Also identified on potsherds dating back as far as 4000 BCE in Palestine, examples of the Pentagram have surfaced in both Egyptian tombs and ancient Sumer dating back to 2700 BCE.

At one time, the Pentagram was a religious symbol in Jerusalem, being the city's official seal between the periods of 300-150 BCE.

The Pentagram was used, by early christians, as a symbol for the five wounds for Christ. Before the cross was introduced, the Pentagram was displayed on amulets and battle gear including the shield of Sir Gawain in the Arthurian Grail romances.

Islam's flag bears the solid, five-pointed star, as well as incorporating the symbology of that number in its five pillars.

According to gnostic teacher Samael Aun Weor, the Pentagram represents humanity's Atman, or Internal Christ.

Today, this symbol is most widely associated with paganism and various schools of occult thought. In these systems the Pentagram is said to express the mind's domination over the elements. This is a continuation of the ancient Babylonian use of the Pentagram symbol as a charm to protect against evil forces.

Heinrich Cornelius Agrippa, among others like Éliphas Lévi, perpetuated the popularity of the pentagram as a magical symbol. In Goethe's *Faust*, the Pentagram prevents the spirit Mephistopheles from leaving a room.

The Pentagram even arises In Japanese culture (五芒星 gobōsei) where it's used as a symbol of magical power representing the five Chinese elements, earth, air, water, wood, metal.

Today, solid five-pointed stars are found on the flags of many nations around the world. In America, the star implies the sovereignty of individual states, also reflecting the sovereignty of Individuals. The Pentagram itself appears on the flag of Morocco where it is said to "represent the link between God and the Nation."

Pythagoras and the sign of the Pentagram

"No one is free who has not obtained the empire of himself. No man is free who cannot command himself."

- *Pythagoras*

> Pythagoras is a mythic character, referred to by his disciples not as Pythagoras but always as "The Master" or "That Man."

Known for their pursuit of truth and knowledge, Pythagorians are said to have used the pentagram as an identifying mark, signing their communications with its sign as a stamp of authenticity.

The Pythagorians called the Pentagram, ὑγιεια, Hygieia or "health." For Pythagoras the connection between proportion, beauty, balance and health was in the design of the Pentagram. In the lines of the Pentagram are symbolic connections to ideas of mathematical perfection via the Golden ratio, or Golden Proportion.

Reflected here is the mathematical key to the kind of divine symmetry and proportion that embodies the Holy Grail of true artists, architects and body-builders.

As a sacred symbol of light, health, and vitality, Pythagoreans taught that the Pentagram symbolizes the fifth element, ether or spirit, which was the basis of vitality and life. In the Pentagram, spirit was exalted in the upright position to distinguish its freedom from, and control over, the four lower elements: fire, water, earth and air, themselves symbols of the four rivers that poured out of the Garden of Eden.

In this regard, the pentad is a symbol of the victory of the aspiring spiritual nature over base material limitations. Ancient philosophers typified this motif in the symbolism of the dragon, whose hidden meaning gives context to the many stories of heroes going forth to "slay the dragon," symbolically driving their sword (the monad) into the body of the dragon (the tetrad).

The tetrad (the elements) plus the monad equals the pentad.

The Pentad, as the union of an odd and an even number (3 and 2) is considered the number symbolic of Nature because when it's multiplied by itself it returns into itself, mirroring the processes of Nature, just as grains of wheat, beginning as seed, fulfill their nature by reproducing and multiplying themselves.

Distinguished by their nature, from other numbers, only 5 and 6 when multiplied by themselves represent and retain their original number as the last figure in their products.

Sometimes referred to as the hierophant, the Pentad is said to represent the "priest of the Mysteries" due to its connection with the spiritual ether. This spiritual ether was said to be Mankind's primary means for attaining mystic development, endowing it with dominion over all superior and inferior beings.

Like many mythic characters, unusual stories attend Pythagoras' birth.

Some stories claim that he was one of the gods taken to human form, incarnating in order to deliver valuable instruction to mankind.

Widely traveled, it is said that Pythagoras was initiated into the mysteries of virtually every great culture of his time.

As the story goes, when he had amassed all the wisdom that Greek culture offered he traveled to Egypt to secure initiation there. From Egypt he traveled to Phoenicia, Syria, the valley of the Euphrates, to Persia where he became versed in the sacred wisdom of the Chaldeans and then into Hindustan to learn from the Brahmins. There it is said he is preserved in record as "the Ionian Teacher."

Among the many claims surrounding his name is that Pythagoras was the first man to call himself a philosopher, which he contrasted with the term "sage," stating that the definition of a philosopher was one who was still attempting to find out.

The philosophical school of Pythagoras was also a series of initiations, teaching moderation in all things, believing that even an excess of virtue was in itself a vice.

One of Pythagoras' central teachings was that both Man and the Universe are made in the image of God, a term sometimes referred to as the *Antropocosmos*.

The ancient wisdom of the Antropocosmos states that both Man and God are made in the same image, and that by understanding one it is possible to possess sacred knowledge of the other.

Central to this cosmic drama is the idea that there is a constant interplay between the Grand Man, or Universe (also referred to as the macrocosm) and Man, the little universe (referred to as the microcosm).

In his teachings, Pythagoras advanced the notion that each creature was stamped with what he termed "a seal"- the dignity of a divinely given pattern like an impression upon the wax of one's physical substance.

In this, is the concept of "character" from the Greek word *kharaktēr* which means "engraved mark," and also "symbol or imprint on the soul."

Phi: Sparks of the Sun

The Pythagorean theorem: $a^2 + b^2 + c^2$ is useful to accurately determine distances between points in a right angled triangle or quadrilaterals whether for constructing monuments, mapping constellations or surveying land. In essence, it describes the fundamental reality of a divine order.

This same principle, it has been found, was used to build Stonehenge, and informed the design of many ancient statues, temples and works of art.

Phi, as the basis for the Golden Ratio can be found throughout the growth patterns of nature, in the Mona Lisa, Taj Mahal, and the construction of the Pyramids. This is the same measure found in the body of Man.

During the European Renaissance the idea of the Golden Proportion was revisited by Italian mathematician Luca Pacioli, one of whose math students happened to be Leonardo Da Vinci.

It was Da Vinci who expressed the idea of the Golden Proportion in relation to the human being in his classic illustration: The Vitruvian Man.

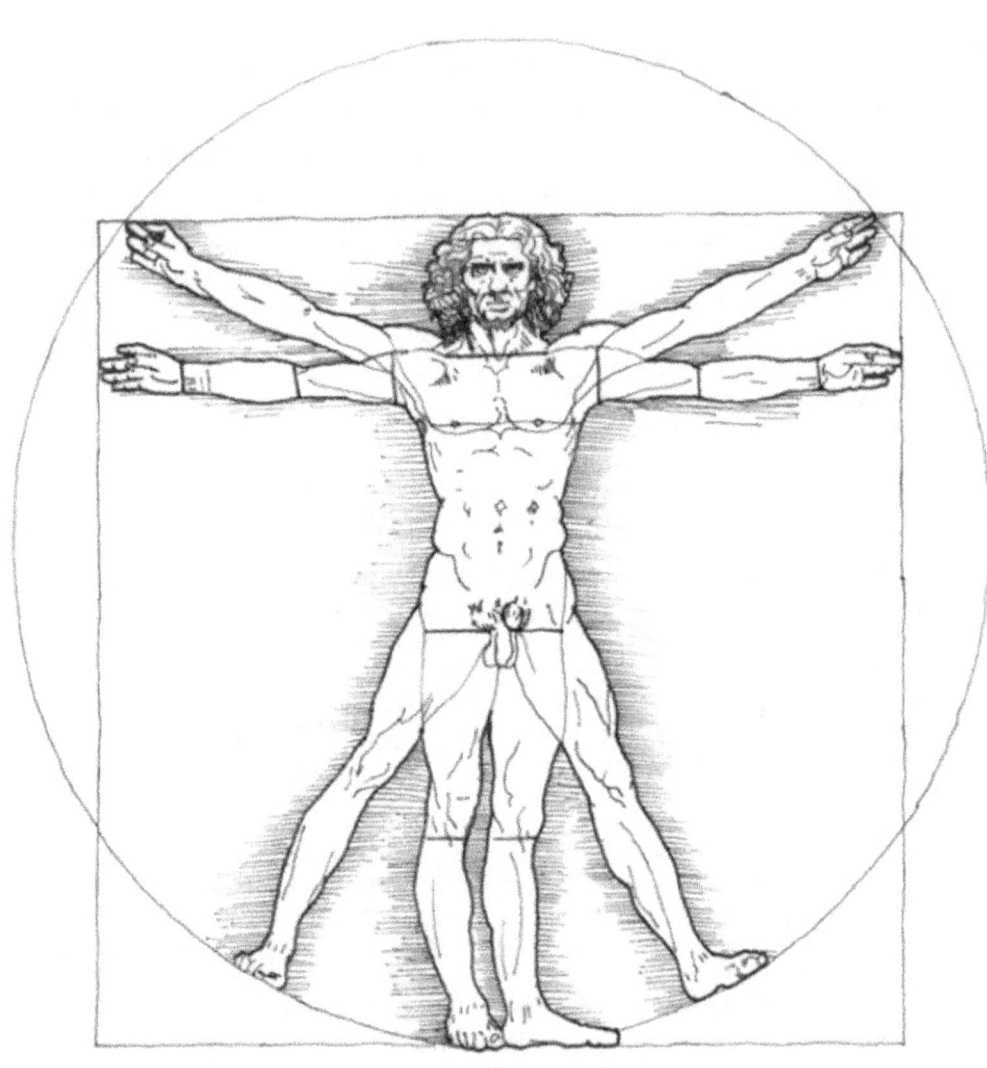

Vitruvian Man, Leonardo da Vinci

Vitruvius:

"For the human body is so designed by nature that the face, from the chin to the top of the forehead and the lowest roots of the hair, is a tenth part of the whole height; the open hand from the wrist to the tip of the middle finger is just the same; the head from the chin to the crown is an eighth, and with the neck and shoulder from the top of the breast to the lowest roots of the hair is a sixth; from the middle of the breast to the summit of the crown is a fourth.

If we take the height of the face itself, the distance from the bottom of the chin to the under side of the nostrils is one third of it; the nose from the underside of the nostrils to a line between the eyebrows is the same; from there to the lowest roots of the hair is also a third, comprising the forehead. The length of the foot is one sixth of the height of the body; of the forearm, one fourth; and the breadth of the breast is also one fourth.

The other members, too, have their own symmetrical proportions, and it was by employing them that the famous painters and sculptors of antiquity attained great and endless renown.

Similarly, in the members of a temple there ought to be the greatest harmony in the symmetrical relations of the different parts to the general magnitude of the whole. Then again, in the human body the central point is naturally the navel. For if a man be placed flat on his back, with his hands and feet extended, and a pair of compasses centered at his navel, the fingers and toes of his two hands and feet will touch the circumference of a circle described therefrom. And just as the human body yields a circular outline, so too a square figure may be found from it. For if we measure the distance from the soles of the feet to the top of the head, and then apply that measure to the outstretched arms, the breadth will be found to be the same as the height, as in the case of plane surfaces which are perfectly square."

— Ten Books on Architecture, Vitruvius

In this book, *The Sun in Man, Secrets of the Royal Art*, the emphasis will be on cultivating those essential qualities traditionally understood to represent the perfecting of the Universal Man.

These are:
* a super-charged Spirit
* a deep Understanding
* a dynamic Will
* a sharp-mind, balanced by Reason
* a foresight into the laws of Cause and Effect
* a calibrated Intuition that leads to Luck or Synchronicity

The aim of this book is to illuminate the Sun in Man as an ancient symbol by "sketching a star" with lines of thought that connect a cross-section of references from ideas to symbols to stories intended to span the distance between the deeply esoteric and the eminently practical.

Man is a Microcosm, or a little world, because he is an extract from all the stars and planets of the whole firmament, from the Earth and elements; and so he is their quintessence.

— *Paracelsus*

CHAPTER ONE

THE DAIMON

The Sun Within

Key Words: The Call, Genius, Character, Self, The Sun-Within

The Ritual: Centralization of the Psyche

Element: Aether/Spirit

In a Deck of Cards: The Aces

In the Tarot: The Major Arcana

Nordic Runes: Sowilo, Elhaz, Eihwaz, Ehwaz, Othala, Mannaz

In Temple Building: The path of the Sun that determines the Temple's orientation.

"The Daimonic is the power of Nature."
— Goethe

"Ethos anthropoi Daimon."
Man's own character is his Daimon.
— Heraclitus

Enter the Daimon:

For many people they'll first notice the close proximity between the word Daimon and demon.

A Daimon, in Greek mythology, refers to a benevolent and noble spirit. For the Greeks, the concept of the Daimon included almost all acts of creativity and power: from prophets to poets, from the artist to the lover. Like the Sun it was the force behind the urge in every Individual to affirm, assert, perpetuate and increase itself. It is this brazen force that emerged from the Crown of the Pharaohs as the uraeus serpent.

The Daimon embodies both Love and Will.

In the words of Diotima, "Eros is a daimon."

In Latin, the daimonic was translated as genii, from which our word "genius" comes. As a concept popular in Roman religion it was this spirit that, for them, explained the source that endowed an Individual with power, manifesting as a particular talent. It is said that this noble spirit presides over one's personal destiny.

In the Kabbalistic tradition this same concept is framed as one's Holy Guardian Angel. Here the concept of angel and daimon become almost interchangeable.

In the words of occultist Aleister Crowley, "The Angel is King, 'the one who can,' the source of authority and the fount of honor. He delivers the enchanted princess (the senses) and makes her his Queen. He is the Ruler, the unconscious WILL."

Heidegger translates the Daimon as an element of consciousness that serves the purpose of pointing or showing. Like the Greek gods, one of its significant characteristics is to give signs and to point in a certain direction.

In the Nordic tradition this is symbolized by the Algiz rune.

It represents an influence pointing to a *Being* beyond the ordinary, an uncanny, ungraspable, unsurpassable force emerging through and from our actions, and like creativity itself, often refusing our control. All this in order to fulfill its purpose of delivering "The Call."

It is this force that drives the Individual in a particular direction, like a personal god giving indications and signs of who we are and what is commanded of us "from up above."

In this sense it is the fountainhead of True Will, the expression of one's divine calling.

In direct juxtaposition is the demonic, as an imbalanced influence, (often imagined as a star with asymmetrical lines and one or more points that extend outside the circumference of its circle).

The demonic represents a force foriegn to the Individual's consciousness and operating behind the lines of its defense. A symptom of demonic force is that it causes its victim to stray from their divine path.

In relation to the Individual's Consciousness, the Daimon is not foreign, it's indigenous and ancestral.

Mandalas:

The symbol for the Daimon is often imagined as a Cryptographic Mandala, (Sanskrit meaning circle) that also contains a quaternity or a multiple of four in some form of a cross, star, square or hexagon.

The image is a synthesis of traditional structure with Individual interpretation.

It is constructed around a central point, to which everything is related, and displays a counterbalanced division of a light half, and a dark half.

We can only perceive forms through light and shadow.

In eastern traditions it has been asserted that "no one mandala is the same as another, all are different because each is a projected image of the psychic condition of its author."

It should then come as no surprise why the mandala would be the supreme symbol of the Individual, or in Jung's conception of Individual "wholeness," as its unified, coherent image.

Simply put, one's mandala is the artistic rendition of "the Sovereign State of Self."

> The mandala is, above all, an image and a synthesis of the dualistic aspects of differentiation and unification, of variety and unity, the external and the internal, the diffused and the concentrated. It excludes disorder and all related symbolism, because, by its very nature, it must surmount disorder. It is then the visual expression of the struggle to achieve order.
>
> - The Dictionary of Symbols, J.E. Cirlot

Jung would call this psychological process "Integration."

> Wholeness or Integration: a condition in which all the different elements of the psyche, both conscious and unconscious, are welded together.
>
> - from The Essential Jung, Integration, Wholeness, and the Self

---

Toward the symbol of the Daimon there is no cautious plea of reconciliation, or low attitude of submissiveness, instead the mirror smiles back: the face of the deity is the wholeness of Man.

Despite that, the spirit of one's Daimon might as well seem like a demon to those who fear the power of inspired individuals.

The Daimon whispers "Live your Will…" and delivers the call for a person to take up a task, for which they alone, live to fulfill.

The bond between the Daimon and the Individual is the bond of commitment, no greater and no less than the wholehearted concentration of one's life and energy to bear upon the destined fulfillment of a mutually shared objective.

Historically, this force and its influence has been responsible for those Individuals and civilizations who rose from oblivion to wield powers beyond every reasonable explanation.

It was the cultivation of this force that made some civilizations rise from mythological mist while others just lingered in that mist. At the most basic level, it is this force and no other that is the source of what one might call Magick.

Goethe spoke of the tremendous power that can emanate from daimonic persons, saying "All united powers do not prevail against them...and they cannot be overcome except by the Universe itself which they have challenged to combat."

Heeding a call from above, the Individual finds that this committed oath to the divine force within them simultaneously breaks the fetters of common convention, shattering those unlawful social contracts that bind the Individual to mediocrity. This freedom allows them full reign, or Sovereign power, to fulfill their destiny.

These Individuals are divinely unbound, and as such, dangerous to those who attempt to bind them.

The Dangers:

The Daimon is dangerous, and yet divine. Divine as a flash of lighting, divine as a call delivered from up-above, divine in that it has no master on Earth.

To some, these divinely inspired Individuals are dangerous for similar reasons.

The call of heaven implies danger and the Daimon is its agent and messenger.

The influence of the Daimon is a danger: to the status quo, to one's own concretized expectations, to growth-stifling rules and regulations, to essential questions gone unasked because the answers were feared, to subjective models of the World that have lost their vitality, to the potential energy contained in a boulder of assumptions precariously poised on a mountain top of popular misconceptions.

The Daimon's natural urge is to give that boulder a nudge. At times the force of one's genius can seem to be mischievous, almost deviant, but ultimately only for the purposes of proving a point or teaching a lesson.

The destructive side of the daimon is only the reverse of its creative side.

The nature of the Daimon is that it contains a paradox that refuses to be fully rational. Its nature is to be uncontained and so it is potentially destructive and creative at the same time.

For many people the word Daimon, which means genius or guiding spirit of fate and character, appears so close to the word demon that it invokes "fears of the devil."

Etymologically, some similarities do exist. The word devil, from the Greek word diabolos, means "to tear apart." From this same origin come words like divorce, divide, diversity and dimension.

These "di" words represent forces whose meaning is to "throw apart unity."

The word Daimon, from the Proto-Indo-European root *dā- means to divide, as in a "part, or portion." It is the Daimon who bridges the divide between heaven and earth, between celestial and mundane affairs. In this respect, the Daimon is the part or *portion of divinity granted to the Individual.*

In contrast to the word diabolic is the word *symbolic* which means to unite or "to bring together." Here we greet the solution to the problem of evil and the "shadow" spoken of by modern psychologists.

To overcome diabolic tendencies, to overcome the forces of internal division and duality that disintegrate and tear apart both psyche and civilization, we must counter this chaos by uniting both light and shadow together, creating a symbolic wholeness of being, a composite of complimenting fire and ice-like tendencies, welding them together in symbol and force – the essence of the Daimon.

This is the ritual referred to as the "Centralizing the Psyche" in *The King's Curriculum, Self-Initiation for Self-Rulers*.

This ritual of Centralizing the Psyche, of bringing together the disperse elements within us, of becoming the light-bearing Sun while also assuming ownership of the shadow that our light invariably casts, is to take to heart Nietzsche's idea of going beyond good and evil, of realizing that the Daimon of our true character is a transpersonal force which cannot be measured in terms of good and evil because, like genius, it transcends both those limitations.

> This is why the rational faculty, or Reason (as the Sword) is but a servant of the WILL – which is the heartbeat of the Daimon – a current of flame flowing from the SUN WITHIN.

Character:

To understand one's Daimon it is necessary to understand one's character.

> Spirit and character are naturally an outgrowth of ancestry and blood.

Embodied in character is one's fate, one's truth, one's calling, and hence the necessity of one's existence.

The Daimon is the divine force which is uniquely yours, your character is its fingerprint and your True Will is its Word.

It is the Logos, or the Word, that gives a meaningful structure to our cosmos. It is this capacity to use the power of words to construct a form that simultaneously allows Man to connect with the Daimon.

With this power, Man possesses the creative ability to construct symbols and myths which, in turn, gives Man the power to construct his own myth, and by proxy, his own image of Self. To wield one's own daimonic power is, ultimately, to be self-creative.

> To know one's calling is to know what one wants MOST in this life.

The Daimon is a bridge between the divine and human, between the subjective and objective worlds, and shares in both. By definition the divine is transcendent and incomprehensible, overcoming duality and its ordinary limitations.

We are expected by contemporary society to be very one-sided, to accept the stamp of one extreme position or another and yet our Daimon takes possession of both poles with such balanced purity that we are able to experience a transpersonal reality that exists above and beyond those limitations.

In the ancient Nordic alphabet, this is represented by the Dagaz rune.

This is an intimate experience that extends to the very ground of our being, encompassing our character, nature and fate. It is the expression of this experience that becomes the source of the Individual's "inner authority."

Wisdom:

The wisdom of the Daimon lies outside one's knowledge base and conventional, theoretical frame. It is unbound by assumptions and expectations.

It represents the divine promethean spark within the Individual, the unapologetic call of the trancedencent heralding the Individual to fully become who they were meant to be.

Still, the totality of this becoming is yet a great mystery.

The philosophical ethics of the Daimon are, by nature of its transcendence, unbound by ordinary limitations.

Descartes said "I think therefore I am."

The Daimon speaks, "I WILL therefore I AM," and before this proclamation all other philosophies fall.

The CALL:

> An inner experience addresses him in an audible voice, saying: "This is what WILL and MUST be." 'If he harkens to the voice, he is at once set apart and isolated as he has resolved to obey the law that commands him from within. His own law! It is the law, the vocation for which he is destined. No more "his own" than the lion that fells him, although it is undoubtedly this particular lion that kills him and not any other lion. Only in this sense is he entitled to speak of 'his' vocation, 'his LAW.'
>
> — Carl Jung

This inner voice speaks of a fuller life, it urges the Individual on to seek a wider, more complete consciousness.

In this quest through darkness an internal friction compounds until finally like the intolerable pressure of some great cosmic event a Sun is born out of sheer need.

Mythologically this is the symbolic birth of the hero at sunrise. For the same reason most heroes, kings and prophets are characterized by solar attributes.

At this act of affirming one's own law, a cosmic clarity of purpose and committed focus are impressed upon the Individual as they become absorbed in their calling.

The Call unites our being and in doing so proves itself to be beyond dualistic limitations. There can be delight in both destructive and creative tendencies so long as they are willed representations of one's immortal "I AM."

Masterful acts of creativity can, at times, be highly destructive.

Reason:

It is true that the force of the Daimon can be very disruptive to the homeostasis of convention. This is the story behind the executions of both Christ and Socrates, they simply embodied a degree of power which made others uncomfortable.

The power of "The Call" is beyond dispute, beyond argument, beyond reason. It looks down upon timid reason from its mighty heights, and like a god with its pointed finger of power presses the stamp of its infinite magnitude upon the finite saying "Reason, you are but a servant, tasked with defending the divine WILL of the Master."

At times, the force of the Daimon can have little concern for reason. It can even take delight in destroying pure rationalist plans, opening the Individual up to creative possibilities that they never knew they possessed.

The spirit of the Daimon can be almost childlike in that it wants what it wants and does not interrogate its own wishes by asking why it desires something or the reason behind its love for a favorite toy.

Ethics:

The ethics of the Daimon are meta-ethics, coming from a realm above and often less human than divine. The Call is the Call, and like orders that descend through a military hierarchy from the General down through the ranks to the lieutenant, the command comes from up above with the only acceptable reply from our lower selves being, "I WILL."

This WILL represents the Individual's very own *living must* and, as such, becomes a matter of necessity.

Contrast this with the notion of free will, the belief in unbound personal choice. However much we may wish to be free, a life bound to no cause leads nowhere. It is the proverbial rudderless ship with no port of destination.

There could almost be a philosophical clash between the concept of free will and True Will if one were to assume that to be free means to be committed to nothing.

Free will supposes a choice, yet if not governed by the personal agency of True Will the variable that determines the context of that choice is missing. Without some context for making a choice the so called decisions made by free will are merely uncoordinated impulses based on no innate intention, no conceived objective. That's where WILL comes in. It acts as the overarching context for making choices. In essence, it symbolizes one's *authority* to do a given thing.

To be governed by one's True Will, the calling of one's Daimon, is to make exactly the choice required by the necessity of one's vision.

Like a carpenter who measures to make cuts, our True Will decisions are like lines marked at exact cutting points, measurements determined by the structure we aspire to build. In this regard, there is great freedom to being committed to the necessity of one's True Will.

According to Plato there are two great cosmic forces operating in the world: Necessity and Reason.

> Reason follows patterns. Its laws are those
> which we can understand.

Necessity is the operation of fate, it's something mysterious, a wandering catalyst current that activates the hidden variables of synchronicity that weave the web of wyrd, the ancient Norse word for fate.

A symbiotic relationship:

The interaction between the Individual and their Daimon is a symbiotic relationship, an intimate partnership of two different, but complementary elements becoming one in function.

Symbolically, its image might be thought of as a God riding on the back of a Beast.

The God part takes the whip and drives the Beast onward, relying on the Beast's strength to make advancement toward a destination that the Beast neither knows nor understands.

With the bit tight in its mouth and the taut leather reins steering the way, the lower part of ourselves is mastered through discipline by the higher part.

Not of its own will alone does the lower part of ourselves simply obey the commands of the Higher Self. It may even do so begrudgingly.

However, without the God part as rider, to drive the lower part of our animal nature onward, that part would remain forever low, unevolved and fatally limited. It would never taste the fruits of completion, never know the higher pleasures offered through the experience of ascendance, never graze the grass of higher celestial pastures.

Yet with appreciable wisdom, the God part of ourselves must also know when to let the whip rest and give the Beast some well deserved grain.

Man is both God and Beast. It is the saddle, the whip and the divine destination that make them one.

The Call of the Daimon can be quite mysterious. At times it is very difficult to understand where the journey is going because it often operates according to a hidden law, above and beyond our conscious capacity to understand, seeming to be governed by a higher objective.

In consideration of societal ethics, the difference between the daimonic and demonic is often little more than the social acceptability of the character values produced by the Daimon in any given time.

There are many values that were once wholly unacceptable in society that are today celebrated, while there are many values once celebrated which are today wholly condemned. Time and place will often determine how one's calling will be received by others. The Daimon has as little concern for disturbing social consensus as an artist has for disturbing the virginity of a canvas.

And yet, the demands of "The Call" <u>must</u> be tempered… by the steel Sword of Reason.

Dreams:

The Daimon commands a space beyond ordinary limitations and yet the manifestation of this superior force must take into account the laws of nature and reason if that force is to be manifest.

We all have drives and dreams of great things we want to accomplish and there's always an element of the fantastic and unrealistic in those dreams, that's their essence. Yet, dreams are the nourishment of Man, they are the prayers of the lower seeking the higher.

Without dreams Man would fall back to dust. Without higher drives Man would have never stood upright.

While all this is true, sensibility warns us at the same time that not all dreams can be fulfilled, not all ambitions can be conquered, at least not in one lifetime.

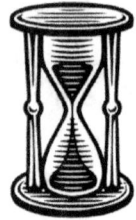

Time:

In this respect, the Daimon might be considered an ancestral spirit bridging the distance between centuries. As Jung put it, the "Spirit of the Depths" bursts through and overcomes the "Spirit of the Times."

Eternity has little concern for the constraints of time. We as Individuals are part of a great chain of events that extends back to the creation of the world. This understanding is reflected in the Jera rune.

In this great chain of events we are called to play an essential part, connecting one chapter with another, one story with another. The call of the Daimon may represent the continuation of a legacy many lifetimes in the making.

A legacy means a Saga that endures for more than one life. In this sense, our communication with our Daimon is like the ancient mind having a dialogue with the modern mind.

Meaning:

The Daimon gives us an answer to our "What" in life.

It informs us, though strong internal drive and conviction, of what we must become, do, and be in this life.

With that authority affirmed, then our reason can guide our "How."

How will we fulfill this drive? How will we overcome the obstacles and challenges that lie between ourselves and our beloved, i.e. the attainment of our ideal aspiration.

Prudence:

This digress was necessary to touch upon one important fact. The force of the Daimon, if untempered by the psychological integrity of a relatively sane character, could lead to mania, psychosis, and insanity.

Yet, a person whose life goes untouched by its Daimon, who is devoid of a higher calling or purpose is doomed to mediocrity no matter how rational, reasonable or cautiously calculated their motives are. They may be a person but they'll never become an Individual.

Heeding the call is a risk, which is why it goes hand in hand with the hero's journey. Heeding the call is a test beyond test, which is why attaining its summit is the ultimate attainment.

Contained within the influence of the Daimon there is a sort of aristocratic dignity for the Individual who bears it because they naturally perceive that all great individuals throughout history have had this same fertilized seed planted in their hearts too - there is a collegium of spirit connected across centuries by the wisdom of the Daimon.

As Goethe states "Some men are chosen to bear it (the Daimon) to a great degree and some are not. Great men who are characterized by the daimonic are invincible until driven by hubris they set their will against nature which is also the nature of the Daimon. This generally proves to be their undoing."

The roadside of this intimately challenging path is strewn with the corpses of those who overestimated or underestimated their abilities, who could not bridge the gap between the higher and lower parts of themselves, who felt the strong invigorating power of the Daimon and then allowed themselves to get carried away by the dopamine-high of manifesting its force.

Chained to rocks on distant, dark mountains are those who have stepped past the threshold of sanity and lost the balance of their minds in an attempt to possess something that was inherently ungraspable, or to do something which was entirely beyond the law that they themselves came to establish.

In short, they coveted the power of the Daimon as a thing in and of itself and strived to use that power outside or beyond their calling. Let their wailing moans be a lesson and a corrective for any such behavior.

The divine force of "The Call" is like a swiftly moving river, there is great power there and also great danger. We want to take advantage of that current, make its strength our strength, use it to generate power and to focus our efforts. We do not want to enter its current in an unfitting canoe only to get swept away by its force and lodged under a bridge somewhere as a drowned and broken casualty.

When we approach the Daimon it's like Ben Franklin flying his kite in the thunderstorm to understand lighting. We can hardly even understand the forces we're provoking, it's all just an experiment. We know lightning exists, we know it's powerful, we just don't yet fully understand how to make practical use of it.

That's what this book is about.

The power of Genius:

SOL SUUS: the Sun Disk, in latin literally, "his own self, the Sun"

The Daimon is a relationship, developed or undeveloped. Ritual is the most ancient technology for developing this relationship.

If we lived in a world where developing the Daimon was a cultural and social responsibility expected of us, then the Ubermensch would become the inevitable result.

Mankind's ultimate evolutionary potential is contained in the generative influence of this force. In this, the Daimon represents the vocation of the Individual's spirit.

> In this vocation of the Daimon, life is the work, the Great Work.

The mistake made in our efforts to understand our calling and our spirit's vocation is often found in the cultural habit of considering it a necessity that one's vocation be exactly the same thing as a job where they earn their bread.

It's wonderful when this happens, but there are times when this will not always be true. In fact, there are many high-callings that have no corporate headquarters. There are many callings that must be fulfilled even without pay.

An Individual who feels an artistic call to be a painter and whose paintings are far ahead of their time may go unappreciated by the paying public, until years after their death.

Yet still, we must honor and bring dignity to what we've been called to do. Instead of pursuing one's calling strictly as a means of wealth we pursue it as a means of expressing our character.

Often an artist who wishes to make money from their art ends up designing corporate billboards.

At its root, character has less to do with the money we earn than our ability to stay true to ourselves despite the pressure to continually yield our character to the so-called necessities of career advancement. In fact, a singular pursuit of wealth often has a corrosive influence on character.

In some sense, we are what we do. But character is more closely related to the way we do something.

The power to act otherwise than the common mass of humanity is a miracle bestowed by the divine spirit of the Daimon and its power. It is the gift of heroes to be endowed with this godlike, supernatural attribute, to be able to go their own way and emancipate themselves from the herd, unfettered by the social risk that accompanies rising up out of unconscious identity with the chains that collectively bind Man to a low and dismal fate.

The attainment of a true and distinguished character is the mark of this vocation. A true vocation is experienced by the Individual as a law delivered from up-above, a law from which there is no escape.

The Individual may browse the pages of history and observe the consistent fact that many an Individual who goes his own way suffers fatal consequences. To the Individual who truly hears the call and feels its necessity, this fact means nothing. The risk is counterbalanced by an intuitive insight into something about which others know nothing. To such an Individual, death becomes no more than a temporary shadow cast by a moving Sun.

One's calling *will*, at last, bring them to that end which is their destiny.

A phrase in this regard is: "If I do what I really must, it will kill me, and yet if I don't, I'll die."

Regardless of the imminent dangers and risk associated with their calling, a higher voice whispers to the Individual insisting that despite the possibility of consequences that no average man could bear, they must yet obey their own law.

Few have the courage or faith to bear the weight of consequence that naturally attends committing to one's own destiny.

There are consequences to any and every form of commitment, both consequences of doing and consequences of not doing.

Sensing this risk, many fail to commit to their destiny while also failing to realize the risk entailed in a failure to commit. The accumulated momentum of this failure to commit to one's calling carries with it a downward spiral whose trajectory leads toward a failure of consciousness of unimaginable magnitude.

Every hazard is a potential victory, every danger is an opportunity to be greater than circumstance. To fail to become is the only failure.

In this same context Christ uttered his famous words, "Forgive them Father for they know not what they do." (Or fail to do)

They have lost contact with their inner voice, and in its place is a group of conventions based on collective necessities. Such lost souls are the money changers of the spirit.

The Greek philosopher Heraclitus said "Character is fate." The author of *The Six pillars of Self-Esteem*, Nathaniel Braden, said "Self-Concept is Destiny."

The similarity here is that who we are naturally determines what we will become. In our nature is our Sovereignty.

Some Individuals possess an innate sense of destiny from an early age while others do not. Some people believe that those who feel a sense of destiny are the chosen stars who stand apart from the masses, and for most of history this has been true.

The reason that some people lack this sense of destiny, this in-born awareness of their personal Daimon, is that early on others interfered with it and their inherited dispositions were just too well-behaved to buck that heavy saddle.

Contemporary culture puts enormous emphasis on being "nice," a word itself derived from the Old French *nice* meaning "foolish, ignorant, frivolous, and senseless," coming from the Latin *nescius* meaning "unaware," or literally "not-knowing." The Daimon is not "nice," it's not a product of contemporary culture, and it can be very indifferent to consensus.

The Daimon is an ancient spirit, one rooted in a primordial reality that extends to the depths of consciousness. Even though the substance of its influence is that of WILL and LOVE, it may yet be a LOVE that to others seems to manifest as a naked WILL-to-power.

Limitations:

A large majority of people are overcome in early life by the pressure of consensus that prevents them from cultivating a relationship with their Daimon. They've been socialized to the point that they quickly prune back any untamed branches, simultaneously limiting the harvest of any fruit that grows outside the lines of clearly established rows.

While some may try to project the stamp of evil upon the Daimon, the real threat it poses is to the demands of society, especially those rigidly imposed upon the Individual when their divine calling ranges into a territory outside of those restrictions.

Many people become so indoctrinated by limits imposed on their consciousness by externally dictated social norms that when they do feel the truth of themselves it feels foreign, taboo to social limitations or frighteningly overpowering in its force. They shade its growth, afraid to let this primordial urge flourish.

It's as if they unconsciously know that if they ever let this genie out of the bottle they may never get it to go back in again, and they're right. Once unleashed, the call of destiny takes on a momentum of its own.

The remaining masses who miss their call are those who lack or never developed the intuitive ability to pick up on the Daimon's subtle prodding influence, guiding them in a specific developmental direction.

When they hear the famous phrase "Know thyself," they simply shrug and reply "What's that supposed to mean? I know myself. My name is Harry."

Such a person misses their call because they have either subconsciously suppressed its influence as a sort of protective mechanism, or simply have never allowed themselves to accept the force of its presence, so they settle for something else.

Such a person fails to commit to the development of their destiny and spirit. They lack the divine inner dialogue that comes from taking communion with their inner fire.

Absent of this, they possess nothing but the monotony of their own mundane inner chatter. Limited as such, their thinking is merely a fractured collection of things they've been told, movies they've watched and advertisements they've subconsciously ingested. Their very words are merely a fractured echo of suggestions they've adopted. They lack authenticity, and so, any real authority.

They lack the certainty that comes with the voice of the Daimon, that voice from upon high, whose words are authoritative in the most sincere meaning of the word.

The fiery oratory of the Daimon lightnings forth like an ancient authority bridging a gap across an impossible expanse of time, yet consistently yielding revelations of something that feels new and unbound.

These revelations come in the form of ideas totally new to the Individual, yet so conceptually well formed that they appear chiseled to perfection by the hand of a superior artist. In simple terms, they are divinity in its most raw form.

Daimon as Genius:

The Daimon is the spirit that brings great ideas.

The Daimon's presence is that feeling one gets when they realize that they're on to something.

> Yeat's described the daimonic as that "other Will," that "dazzling, unforeseen wing-footed wanderer" – a force outside himself which was at the same time oriented to his personal being.
> - *Rollo May, Will and Love*

The Daimon has, throughout history, been referred to by a variety of names. The Greeks referred to this transcendent influence as a person's Daimon. The Romans called this genius. The judeo-christian traditions refer to this as one's Holy Guardian Angel. To new age followers the spiritually stripped down term Higher Self is often used.

> "In Plato, a familiar Genius accompanies Man at his birth, follows and watches him all his life, and at death conducts him to the tribunal of the Great Judge. These Genii are the media of communication between Man and the Gods; and the soul is ever in their presence. This doctrine is taught in the oracles of Zoroaster; and these Genii were the intelligences that resided in the planets."
>
> - Albert Pike, Morals and Dogma

Whatever we desire to call this influence, it represents a hard to pin down psychological fact. It is the lifeblood of one's heart-calling, both a personal imaginal spirit and also the spinning wheel of one's own fate.

It is the fate we carry within us, carried in our character and expressed as our own particular form of genius. The Daimon might be thought of as a separate being that accompanies, guides, protects and warns us along our journey.

The Daimon is our Inner Initiator, our teacher and guide. No one really teaches themselves anything they don't know and yet this is what seems to be happening with the Inner Initiator, one comes to discover that they know a great deal more than they think they know, that they are a great deal more than they think they are.

Innate knowledge, or even secret knowledge, is the unique expression of the Daimon. The Daimon manifests as a divine flame of inner knowing that brings with it an inner fervor. It is from the fire of this inner fervor that the Individual's torch of self-actualization ignites.

It is knowledge of one's Daimon and its illuminating influence which is the fire that ignites our torch, and by the light of this torch we are drawn deeper into the labyrinth of knowing ourselves, guided through this maze of self-actualization by the guidance of our Daimon.

In seeking this knowledge we enter upon a mythic path, the same as tread by Odin, the archetypal God of WILL.

In seeking this knowledge we drink from the well of Mimir. We become suddenly aware of the web of fate whose threads have woven together the disparate and seemingly unconnected events of our lives.

As we step back to observe the tapestry of our Saga our minds naturally are drawn to that final knot, that culmination of the whole work, the end, the conclusion, the finality, and its fateful word: Success.

The word success can never be entered into our book of life unless it's the last word. Before that, its use would be preemptive and disconcerting.

The Daimon offers the Divine Cup, whispering "Drink, know thyself." Knowing, of this degree, comes with an unforeseen catch – the weight of responsibility.

Once we know, we cannot un-know, however much we try. Once we hear the call, there is no going back. Once we drink from the cup of understanding, and taste that bittersweet beverage, we are forever changed.

The Hero is the one who has the courage to face reality.

Knowledge is the death of innocence.

This brings us to an important consideration: How much knowledge can one bear, and live?

To come to know too much too soon has broken many otherwise strong Individuals.

If we desire to know then we must be prepared to take responsibility for that knowledge. In taking responsibility we are also called to take action.

Once we "know" then our WILL is fertilized, activated to express our direct response to that knowing.

Like Odin's awakening at the well of Mimir, we too awaken when we drink from the Daimon's Cup of Gnosis.

Like Odin, when he received the power to see past, present and future only to witness the fateful conclusion of Ragnarok and his own brutal death in the jaws of the terrifying Fenris Wolf, we too receive the conclusive knowledge of our own beginning and ending. The serpent's tail comes right back around into its mouth.

Knowledge informs us but it does not make us immune from its ultimate consequence.

"How terrible it is to know when no good comes from knowing," are the haunting words of Tiresiasto to Odedipus.

Odin might have felt the same when his sip from the well confronted his conscious awareness with his subconscious knowledge of Ragnarok.

Yet, rather than cowering from this imminent fate, Odin made his conscious existence a commitment to eventually greeting this event head on.

Fate had decreed that Ragnorok would be a battle that could not be won, and yet rather than merely submitting to that dire decree Odin set himself the task of organizing his efforts so as to put his own spin on fate.

He perceived that while some aspects of fate were final, others could be maneuvered toward a result more in conformity with his higher Will.

Rather than submit to Mimir's divination, Odin set himself to an archetypally magical task, he reframed defeat into victory. He accomplishes this by tending the outcome of that battle so that he can transform the underlying narrative of life from a catastrophic ending (the death of God, meaning and order) into a final alchemical clash (Ragnarok) that neutralizes all warring opposites in order to transform the bloody battlefield of Asgard into a fertile ground for the eventual rebirth of order, light and hope in a New God Image. There's something deeply alchemical in this tale.

Oedipus said "I will not stop till I have known the whole."

We walk the path of destiny when we, like Odin, commit to our own saga of completion.

At this conclusion there is a spiritual marriage celebrated on the inner planes. Two seemingly different parts of oneself, the conscious self and the Daimon, find that they are indeed wed to one reality and one fate, and accepting this fact they become sealed by vow to become, in essence, ONE WILL.

In this, it is not the higher part of oneself that wishes to become the same as the lower. That would be a step down. Rather it is the lower aspiring to the higher. The Daimon is the infinite in oneself wishing to retrieve the finite in oneself.

In this task the Daimon is the archetypal savior, redeeming consciousness from the fetters of finite limitation and its inevitable conclusions – conscious death.

The Daimon is the blueprint and architect of our completed consciousness, while what we generally call our "self" is the pile of material from which the work will be accomplished. In psychological terms, the Daimon is the way we encounter the initiatory hall of our unconscious, and our conscious personality is the sacrifice, or price we pay, to enter in through that great gate.

In the beginning, the Daimon is not ourself and we are not yet the complete embodiment of our Daimon. There must first be a bridge built between the two. The Daimon is not quite what we regard as ourself and so the new age term Higher Self is lacking in this regard. One's Daimon is closer to their immortal "I AM," and its Will-to-become, than just an idealized version of one's social personality.

The Daimon is separate and yet there is a symbiotic relationship between the Daimon and the Individual. It has its own source and brings its own legacy, as a cup from which we drink. Its history is independent from one's own, and yet its incarnation through one's own words and deeds adds to its history as the two become one. The Daimon is the divine force working with us, through us and for us, as the messenger of an agenda delivered from up-above.

The relationship between the Individual and the Daimon is one of interdependence. It is the seeking of harmonization between the Will of the Individual and what Yeats called "that other Will," which represents one's awareness of the Daimon.

Harmonization of these two factors is born from the sublime realization that this is a relationship in the truest sense of the word, one where the fulfillment of each can be achieved only through the other.

A Daimon in the ancient world was a figure from somewhere else, neither human nor god, but rather something between the two. Like the Jinn in Arabic lore, it represents an entity belonging in a middle region between Heaven and Earth, translating higher currents into frequencies relatable to human incarnations.

As an intermediary spirit between the gods and the human self the Daimon brings messages from the throne of the most high and delivers them across the abyss to the ear of the incarnated representative embodied by the Individual.

In this symbiotic relationship, we choose our Daimon as our Daimon chooses us. In this regard we all select our lot in life.

When we express our character, we express our Daimon and in doing so we accept and embrace our lot in life.

This is in close proximity to what Fredrick Nietzche termed "Amor Fati," or love of fate. If character is destiny and destiny is fate, then our Daimon is our character and the acceptance of our character in faith is the full expression of Amor Fati.

> This means accepting our True Will and everything that comes with it.

Character refers to the deep structures of our unconscious identity, cornerstones of our pyramid of consciousness that are almost entirely resistant to change.

These cornerstones of character represent the foundation of our enduring Self, our immortal "I AM." These hard to change lines of fate are like the lines in our palm. Similarly, our fingerprint is the signature of our Daimon.

You find your genius by looking in the mirror and seeing the themes of your life reflecting back at you.

The etymology of the word "character" connects it with a marking instrument. This is the hand of character as it scribbles its story upon one's own book of life.

Our character is the mark of our Daimon. In turn, our force of character becomes the mark we make on life.

The art of True Will means taking up the creative responsibility to "carve for oneself," to insure that no writing in the book of our lives is arbitrary, to insure that every word of every chapter can be interpreted as having a decided purpose.

Eudaimonia:

Eudaimonia contains the word Daimon, and is a Greek word that translates as happiness. Man is most happy when he is following his own way, following the calling that emerges moment by moment from within.

Eudaimona is the feeling we get when the call of our Daimon is unobstructed. In the Nordic alphabet this is symbolized by the rune Wunjo.

Psychologists and high-performing Individuals might refer to this same feeling as "flow."

The relationship between oneself and one's Daimon is symbiotic. The Daimon bestows the blessing of an inspired calling, guiding, protecting and initiating the Individual through an intimate knowledge of a deeper vein of subconscious power operating within them.

The Individual, in turn manifests the force of their Daimon through word and deed. This relationship can aptly be termed spiritual in every conceivable sense of the word.

The Individual hears a call upon high, something alluringly mysterious and profoundly familiar and then actively responds to a deep desire to fulfill it.

Once again, the Daimon is of a higher level than one's ordinary, everyday consciousness. It's fiery inner oratory lightnings forth from a place un-oppressed by mere mundane concerns. Its influence is more directed toward the legacy of one's immortal "I AM" than of the ordinary worries which consume most common lives.

We may find, at times, that the Daimon seems to have little concern for our stagnant comfort or desire for blanket security. Like the Gnostic god Abraxas, with whip in hand, it drives our spirit forth toward the completion of our consciousness, toward the fulfillment of our legacy.

We can look at the lives of almost any great individual and see this. How many could have stopped and rested on their laurels and early accomplishments and lived lives of ease and security, yet instead they felt compelled to abandon themselves to destiny, and in doing so won the greatest prize of all – the metaphoric bronze statue of immortality.

For many people, thoughts like this seem like egotism and a "better than thou" approach to life. Yet, it is the Individual who religiously unites with their Daimon who in turn distinguishes themselves from the ordinary masses.

This communion with one's Daimon is the bread and wine of prophets. It is the influence of genius that makes one Individual unequal to another.

The Star of One's Destiny:

> "While the early American founders like Thomas Jefferson were deeply influenced by Greek ideas, they also suffered spiritually from the Age of Reason into which they were born. Many men of the so-called 'Enlightenment' were deeply troubled by Socrates' daimon. They attempted to suggest that Socrates was really either simply referring to Prudence or his conscience or that he was just guilty of ancient superstitions. Socrates did not mean Prudence or conscience and he was the least superstitious man imaginable."
>
> - Rollo May, *Will and Love*

Despite being "men of reason" the words of both the Declaration of Independence and the Constitution bear the mysterious trademark of the Daimon - brilliance combined with eloquence.

Not only do these documents show every indication of being the channeled intelligence of the daimonic, they bear the signatures of more than one daimonically inspired Individual. The founding fathers were "following their own star," and that theme became the unconscious tagline of everything truly American. A few years later, across the ocean, the French Revolution was similarly inspired.

The momentum of that revolution was spearheaded by the mighty genius of Napoleon, a man who followed "his own Star" above all else, a phrase he often used. Napoleon was an Individual whose power was derived from a total commitment to his "Star."

It was by this star that his guiding torch was lit, and by its light he drove himself forth through unimaginable danger and peril completely driven by faith in destiny.

Some will no doubt argue that Napoleon was not a "good" person, but none can argue that his incarnation forever altered the course of history and the events in which he participated possessed so much synchronicity to make it appear that he was chosen by a higher force to play the role he did on history's stage.

Rollo May in his book *Will and Love* states that:

"Goethe, who described himself as having discovered the daimonic very early in his career, was continually enthralled by the daimonic, suggesting that its greatness consisted of being *at the right place at the right time.*

Carl Jung called this same phenomenon "Synchronicity."

In Geothe's autobiography he states, "Although the daimonic can manifest itself in the most remarkable way even in some animals, it primarily is connected with Man. It represents a power which is, if not opposed to the moral order of the world, is yet at cross-purposes to it.

In the most awesome form the daimonic appears when it manifests itself in some human beings. They are not always men superior in mind or talents, seldom do they recommend themselves by the goodness of their heart. Yet a tremendous power emanates from them, they possess an incredible force over all other creatures and even over the elements; nobody can say how far their influence will reach."

By the mysterious force of their Daimon, Individuals can and do forge themselves toward some glory that is both higher than, and unequal to, the low-watermark of expectations generally accepted by the mass of humanity.

It is not a mountain peak but a swamp of mediocrity that most of humanity experiences as everyday life.

The fact that some have managed to rise above this swamp, have been able to ascend above the common place, to become something more than human in relation to ordinary human limitations is a fact of history, and one for which we should be grateful.

It is a historical fact that the deeds that define our conceptions of the potential greatness of mankind, all those lofty spiritual aspirations, liberating deeds, and monumental achievements of world history that fundamentally distinguish mankind from the animals in the field, have sprung from these kinds of leading personalities and never from the timid, inert mass.

The world is moved by the light of genius.

Human history would be nothing more than a long monotonous chronology of mouths to feed, asses to wipe and graves to dig if its book did not possess these rare, intermittent pages dogeared with the extraordinary deeds of extraordinary Individuals.

In Jung's view, "Nature is aristocratic, and one person of value outweighs ten lesser ones."

Yet all that being true, it is obvious that for the sake of a stable society it's also necessary that all Individuals be provided with a strong sense of being equal *before the law.*

That accomplished, it would do us well to acknowledge that the presumption of absolute equality in life is entirely foreign to nature herself. No river is equal to another river, no mountain is equal to another mountain, each is undeniably its own testament to the laws of its creation.

We might add that no Daimon is equal to another.

We must, as a means of civic preservation, seek to preserve equality before the law, while also recognizing and even embracing the fact that Individuals are supremely unequal, which is the very thing that makes them Individuals.

This means acknowledging that the jurisdiction of one's power, and the measure of one's attainments, are a function of one's own Daimon and an expression of one's own innate character. Individuals are, ultimately, limited only by the limitations of their own original genius.

Much of this comes down to the question of whether the Individual accepts their destiny, is willing to play its role, and accepts its necessary sacrifices.

"Every man is an actor of his own ideal."
- *Fredrick Nietzsche*

For the Individual with the courage to heed the guidance of their own star this means awakening to the original seed of one's soul and hearing it speak.

This seed has an agenda. It pushes, leads, guides, and directs us toward the fruition of our potential like the Sun guides the growth of a tree to produce its fruit.

To see this tree produce its inevitable fruit, one must possess a religious fidelity to the law of their own being.

To persist in this endeavor means possessing a trust in this law that solidifies as a *faith*. It requires a loyal perseverance through obstacles and ordeals with an unconquerable confidence born from an attitude as if one's calling was ordained by the highest God.

To begin this journey the Individual consciously initiates a commitment to choose their own way by a deliberate and willing sacrifice of all others ways: whether of a moral, social, political, religious or philosophical nature.

This wisdom has a long tradition of being the way of the few, and elect.

Back to the earliest times this strange adventure of consciousness has been the way of mankind's most legendary heroes, those who chose not to run away from the final consequence of their being.

This is the way of the true "Suns of God," those legendary Heroes, Prophets and Kings, whose names perish not.

The vast majority of mankind is easily deterred from choosing their own way.

They unwittingly renounce their own wholeness for convention and, in doing so, they sacrifice the fortune of their Individual character and inheritance of their destiny in an act of submission to a collective mode of existence.

To be without a Daimon is to be damned to a fate of mediocrity. Anyone who feels the call to escape the prison of mediocrity hears the call of their Daimon.

The call is to take flight on the wings of the Daimon, to soar, to conquer, to (in Nietzsche's own words) slay the dragon who on every scale is written the words "thou shalt." This is especially true when those "thou shalt" statements bind the Individual to an inauthentic path.

There is a sort of dignity demanded of us by our Daimon as we create our own cosmos according to the splendor of its vision.

To give life to one's Daimon is to possess a fire in the eyes, to be lit-up by the Sun Within, to light the torch of destiny and boldly carry it forth with the full acceptance of all that fate may bring.

The Rod of True Will becomes this Torch, a guiding light through the darkness of a fatally meaningless and uncertain existence.

The WILL is a flame lit by the Sun Within.

The torch of True Will becomes the carrier of this divine flame. The ritual of words and deeds performed in the service of this flame are the manifest expressions of its light, a solar gift to the world.

In this sense, our calling represents the light that shines from us, and through us.

When we incorporate the power of the Daimon, we forge an intimate connection with it and in doing so we make it personal.

It becomes us just as we become it.

It comes to constitute our own "center," our SUN WITHIN. It becomes the Solar Light of our inner cosmos, the very source of our Individuality and as such the source of Light, and Love, and Life.

Living for our calling and having a mission of purpose is both an in-pouring of blessing to us from above and also an outpouring of blessing from us to the World.

One's calling is like the nourishment of one's spirit. One's character is the manifest fingerprint of one's Daimon. One's WILL is the measure of how they encounter the obstacles that lie between them and what they aspire to become.

Initiation has "lighting this torch" as its core objective. This means not only lighting the Torch but keeping it lit and if it goes out to be able to light it once again.

As children we are all initially born with this torch burning bright. To relight it time and time again is the role of initiation. To keep it burning is the role of Ritual.

To keep this fire burning is a great devotion, a statement equally true of both love and life.

Be lamps unto yourselves.

Be you a refuge unto yourself.

Take to yourselves no other refuge.

Buddha, just before he died

Tools of the Royal Art:

The Symbol of the Daimon is: the Sun, or in ritual as a lamp or light hung above the altar. A solar symbol is often conceived to represent the spirit of one's Daimon. This symbol forms the design of a sigil to be turned into various forms of art as a sort of monogram, mandala, or combination of symbolic features converging on a central point.

Ritual Practices:

The Ritual of the Daimon is a three-part ritual, reflecting the phases of a chess game.

There are beginning game, middle game, and end game phases of the Ritual of the Daimon. It begins as a ritualized phase of destruction, destroying an old conceptual limitation of self. It then advances to a phase of Self-Discovery, symbolized by the climbing of the Primordial Mountain. During this ritualized climb one is simultaneously "building one's pyramid." This ritual is directed towards the establishment of a new hierarchy of consciousness within. This ritual culminates as a sense of internal "checkmate," when the higher self asserts its unquestionable dominance over the lower self. This is simultaneously the emergence of sovereign consciousness — a victory over darkness, disorder and chaos, by the light of genius.

Mantra: Divine words of Power.

The Word gives man power over the daimonic. This Word is communicated, in its original, powerful form through symbol and myth. This divine Word, which connects one with their Daimon, grants the power to change one's image of Self by becoming the author of one's own Myth.

Sometimes a single word suffices, but often it is better expressed through a short phrase or formula. The words or phrases to be used naturally differ and must be chosen in accordance with the objective as the force to be evoked and developed.

To develop this force, what one wills to accomplish may need to be reaffirmed as a subconscious command, or mantra, a great many times.

The number of repetitions required will depend on the aim's proximity, the difficulty of its attainment, and the necessary time required for the process of manifestation to complete itself.

This mantra, or command, is then hammered home through repetition, charged with the spirit of a persistent, invincible, inner-affirmative attitude.

The creation of a Sigil / Personal Symbol:

Task: Articulate symbolically the full nature of your Daimon, conceiving a form that conveys the symbolic interest, or "light" of your Daimon.

The role of the Daimon is to bring together opposing forces that exist within the Individual and to unite them.

To this end, connect these opposing forces in a coherent and balanced symbol, so that both forces may drive one's chariot of consciousness toward a unified destination.

Practical Matters:

The practice of Amor Fati.

In psychological conceptions, the Daimon might appear like a one of those mythic, composite beasts of ancient lore, having the head of Carl Jung's conception of "Self," with a body composed of unconscious, symbolic structures, and bearing Freud's "libido" like Zeus with his lightning bolt.

> "Man doth not live by bread alone, but by every word that proceedeth from the mouth of God."

Man is not made for material concerns alone. Basic survival is not enough to fulfill Man's spirit. Given breath and life by the divine, Man is to be nourished by every word, insight, and inspiration that the Daimon delivers from heaven's heights.

> These flashes of insight are the current of life and light.

> Communion with one's Daimon represents the act of spirit meeting Earth.

CHAPTER TWO

THE TRUE WILL

The Father of Creation

Key Words and Phrases: Will, Libido, Life, Rod, Drive, Urge, Call, Destiny

Ritual: putting a ring on the branch, "Sol Oath"

Element: Fire

Suit in cards: Clubs

Tarot: The Wands

Nordic Runes: Wunjo, Ansuz, Fehu

Temple Building: the Upright column, Perpendicular lines

"...it seems to me above all necessary to declare here who and what I am."

– Nietzche, Ecce Homo

The Will to Life:

The Will is the Individual's own branch from the Tree-of-Life.

Traditionally it is a rod of wood, sometimes illustrated as a budding branch.

This image conceptualizes the WILL. It represents one's "Will-to-life." This means it is also the Will-to both growth and development.

It represents the original, organic-driver of consciousness, the primal libido of one's innermost nature, the truest, most sincere expression of the wildness of one's character.

The WILL is the active aspect of our being, our energized enthusiasm to perform certain acts and, through those acts, to connect with certain experiences.

One's WILL is the current of energy that streams from one's central source of consciousness, the light-bearing SUN WITHIN.

As such, the WILL is the basis of our internal LAW. It is the "ruler" of our consciousness and the measure of our aspiration.

Alan Watts once commented that "Law is a way of measuring what happens," and this also applies to True WILL which is the yardstick or royal cubit that acts as the unit of measure that guides the construction of our temple of consciousness.

In action, the WILL is the bringer of motion, it is the lever to a fulcrum, a multiplier of force aimed upward, a WILL to "rise above."

The WILL is the dynamic aspect of the creative SELF. No amount of belief is valid without action. The WILL represents action consistent with conviction.

Behind all of life's creative efforts is an act of WILL.

It is the hidden life of physical life, representing the Individual's unity of effort, the consolidation of one's FORCE toward a given END.

It is a developed WILL that improves the effectiveness of all endeavors. In order for this to be true, the WILL must be "true."

TRUE WILL represents a truth embodied in the Individual's character, a truth supported by mental states and beliefs. It is a truth confirmed and reaffirmed through ritualized intent.

The highest Individual is one who trusts their own genius. To trust one's own genius is also to trust its expression: the True WILL.

The True WILL represents the voice, or Word, of one's Daimon.

The True WILL is the vital impulse inherent in the Individual's natural character, what psychologists sometimes refer to as one's *Natural Lead Function*. Freud coined the related phrase *libido* to describe the force behind the psyche's will-to-action.

Jung added to this by commenting on how this power may mysteriously become infused, and held, in ritual objects – a term which he called *mana power*.

The Function of the Will

Through modern, technological knowledge mankind has made itself into a "magician," at least in material terms.

Yet, even as mankind has acquired this knowledge, and along with it an impressive degree of power over nature, mankind's knowledge and control of itself and its inner being is frail.

Even with mankind's ability to descend to the depths of the ocean and send rockets up toward the stars, the human creature still suffers from an ignorance of what is going on in the depths of its own unconscious.

The vast majority of mankind is largely unaware of its ability to reach the higher, luminous spheres of its own superconscious. For this lack, most Individuals in the human race live an existence largely unaware of these potentials. Most never become aware of the rightful jurisdiction of their True Self.

Ironically, mankind now lives on the precipice of becoming the victim of its own achievements. Presently, mankind is in imminent danger of losing control of the tremendous technical forces at its disposal.

In a world that moves on with increasing momentum, speed and complexity, it is ironic but not surprising that a simplification of Man's outer life is now necessary if the species is to regain its balance. It must begin by allowing room for the development of those other, inner powers, hidden within consciousness.

It is the development of these inner powers that will lead Man to realize the potency of its own transcendent WILL and, in doing so, to realize the potent role offered to it within the order of the cosmos.

The True WILL holds a central position in Man's consciousness. It possesses an intimate connection with the core of his being – the Sun Within.

This Sun Within is Man's connection to the inner cosmos, and by proxy, the cosmos itself. This is the "as above, so below principle" at work.

This is the magic of the Anthropo-Cosmos.

When the WILL becomes connected to the greater processes in this way, it arouses a strong incentive within the Individual to rise to life's peak, building from a firm foundation in natural law for the purpose of constructing its pyramid of transcendent meaning.

In the first stages, the Individual recognizes that a higher WILL does indeed exist, and that *it is* the creator of the World.

The second stage involves the Individual's realization of having a personal WILL themselves, and in this, a sense of sharing in the creator's power.

The third stage commences when the Individual conceives of these two WILLs as sharing an intent, of being ONE in essence.

This involves a peak-experience. The Individual gets the sense of being a WILL, of becoming fully identified with that WILL, and through that relationship, of becoming an elemental force of nature.

Once the Individual becomes conscious of the WILL's nature and function, the next step is in deciding what is to be done, how this force will be brought through to manifestation.

This means applying the Royal Art and commanding all the means necessary for the WILL's realization.

In this, the Individual takes up the heroic stance toward life, persisting in their chosen task in the face of all ordeals, opponents, obstacles and difficulties.

This means overcoming various forms of resistance.

These come in the form of inner impulses or external influences whose friction tends toward inertia and a slowing of the WILL's progress.

It is with these forces that the Individual must do battle, never allowing themselves to be dominated by circumstance.

With True WILL as the guiding compass, the Individual becomes captain of the ship, the helmsman who understands what the appropriate course of the ship must be and keeps it steady through waves, winds, and currents.

The Oath

Affirmation is a pivotal stage in the act of willing.

Once the stages of deliberation, choice, and decision have been carried through, there comes the phase of commitment, so that what is willed shall: be, happen, or manifest itself.

The first step is affirmation.

The WILL is the power of affirming or denying.

The word POWER means two things, power in the sense of capacity, and power as potency or energy.

So, what then is implied, and required, by volitional affirmations, or the affirmative WILL?

Fundamentally, it is born of a sense, or state of mind: of *certainty*.

This comes from the synthesis of two inner attitudes: faith and conviction.

> True faith is by nature intuitive.

It perceives the reality of what is not evident, not manifest, and accepts it.

In St.Paul's words it is the "substance of things hoped for, the evidence of things not seen."

There can hardly be a more magic-oriented quote.

To be effective, affirmation must not only be vigorous, it must possess a strong dynamic potential, or intensity.

"The Call" of Authority:

Affirmation may be considered a *command*, a command given with Authority.

Authority may proceed from a position of responsibility to some function in the external world, but it is especially and essentially an inner quality, an inner reality, psychological or spiritual.

Whoever exercises it feels, indeed knows, that he possesses it, and those to whom it is directed perceive it directly.

This Authority can, and indeed should, be exercised particularly on the psychological energies, and functions within us, that we need to achieve our purpose.

In order for the WILL's positive, creative function to propel the Individual forward and enable them to confidently persist onward despite the slings and arrows of outrageous fortune, the WILL must be strong.

In order to develop this strength to persist in the face of strong contrary inclinations the Individual must understand their True WILL to be necessary, a *living must*.

In its ontological aspect, the True WILL represents the development of the Individual's own "living must" because the growth implied in True WILL deals directly with the nature and being of the Individual themself.

This means that their WILL is supported not only by strong beliefs and desires but also by the current of force that represents their innermost being or character, brought to life by the Daimon.

This development is all the better when these beliefs and desires are both strengthened and given momentum by ritual.

This momentum allows for resolutions to become stronger than any contrary desires. This means cultivating a WILL that possesses the power of conviction and confirming that conviction with a resolute OATH, one firmly made so that reconsideration is silenced.

The Joy of Will

The WILL represents the satisfaction of the Individual's highest need, motivated by their deepest intuition. This represents the relationship between the Rod and Cup.

"Enjoyment" is the result of the satisfaction of a need. For each of the levels of needs there is a corresponding kind of enjoyment.

The result of satisfying the basic needs is called pleasure. The general subjective state whose normal needs are temporarily satisfied can be called happiness.

Transpersonal self-realization, (The Holy Grail) and the satisfaction of the highest needs of consciousness, also called *self-actualization*, represents the achievement of communion or identification with universal reality. Mystics refer to this state as "bliss." This manifests when there is a harmonious union between the personal and the transpersonal WILL.

At its height, the Royal Art includes the satisfaction of all levels of these needs.

Dimensions of the Will

The WILL possesses different dimensions that manifest as various modes of expression of the WILL-in-action.

First, the Individual grasps the sublime truth that at the core of their essential being is a WILL that manifests as a "willing self."

The expression of this WILL then develops through stages, outlining a process or manifestation of that WILL, as it unfolds from beginning to end.

In order to accomplish the completion of this process the WILL must be trained to persist with concentrated effort over the long haul. This implies the possession of a "strong WILL."

So rare is the development of a complete WILL, with so few applying their energy to its development in a dedicated and consistent way, that the Individual who develops their WILL is often capable of using this power to overcome the weakened wills of others.

History's pages are highlighted by this type of Individual: one who simultaneously dares everything and fears nothing.

However, the development of "strength of the WILL," is only one part of the equation of an effective WILL. The other aspect is "the skillful WILL."

Like the guile of the mythic Odysseus, this means cultivating the ability to apply one's energy artfully and skillfully to situations in order to obtain the maximum attainment with the least possible expenditure of time, energy and resources (Strategic WILL).

Developing skill in relation to WILL means the Individual must deeply understand their own inner constitution in order to activate the full force of WILL.

They must feel their WILL to be fulfilling.

To stimulate this dopamine response the Individual must understand their WILL as the path toward the fulfillment of "higher needs."

Keeping in alignment with their inherent constitution, the Individual is able to utilize those aspects of themselves that already have the tendency to produce the specific action or condition they are aiming for.

In time, this process leads to the realization of the Transpersonal WILL, that summit of revelation which leads to the sacralization of the Individual's everyday life.

Qualities of the Will

In traditional symbology the WILL represents the element of fire.

Its qualities are intense energy and a dynamic expression of power in acts of initiative, courage and daring.

This means the ability to concentrate our energy and focus with a sort of one-pointedness of attention over the long haul, funneling this energy with disciplined control toward the ultimate objective in pursuit of mastery.

The result of all control, discipline, and training is the achievement of mastery, which gives the Individual both maximum effectiveness and the most intense and enduring sense of meaning, satisfaction, and joy.

Along the way, at important crossroads, this will require a prompt, resolute decisiveness. Some paths will abruptly dead end, change direction, turn back on themselves or otherwise seem to lead to a difficult impasse. In these moments the Individual must be willing to firmly wield the Sword, that's to say, to be able to decide. Failure to decide leads to stagnation.

Not to decide is also a decision.

For certain tasks of great length, steadfastness of purpose and persistence are needed even more than energy. This involves the kind of persistence exercised in spite of repeated failures, sometimes called tenacity. There is a Latin saying that relates to this "the drzop of water makes a hole in the stone not through force but by its constant falling."

This persistence manifests as endurance, the ability to endure, the willingness to accept pain. In this regard one might consider that to experience pain in life is unavoidable, but to "suffer" is a choice. That's one of the great advantages of the hero's journey – it makes both our joys and pains holy.

Organization and Synthesis

While concentration generally, and especially at first, requires a definite act of WILL, after some time it can persist on its own without any effort or tension of the WILL itself.

There is another and higher condition in which the personal WILL is effortless; occurring when the willer is so identified with the Transpersonal WILL that their activities are accomplished with free spontaneity. In the eastern traditions this touches upon the concept of Wu-Wei.

In this state, one feels they have become a willing channel into, and through which, powerful energies flow and operate.

The WILL contains two functions: one-pointed attention and inhibition. These are the gas and brakes of self-control.

The WILL is a force that moves, but its power can also be summoned to *resist* certain non-compliant urgues. This power, called inhibition, represents a temporary check of reflex actions.

Deeply embedded in the chronicles of "Mankind's Mythic Saga of Willed Action," are the repeated roles of some of its central characters, namely: Risk, Courage, Daring, and Initiative.

The hero's journey begins, right out of the gate, with a confrontation with danger. To continue on, undeterred by this fact, means the recognition, and acceptance, that full and lasting security in this world is fundamentally an illusion.

At the same time, risk has its incentives, often bringing with it a feeling of intense aliveness and clarity, and a subsequent stimulation of one's courage and WILL by some law of deeply inherited, instinctual necessity.

Stragenomics: Strategy and Economics

To be effective, our WILL must demonstrate a balance of activity both internal and external in the form of coordination and cooperation.

A powerful WILL, as the central component, or axis, of our inner cosmos, is the Individual's demonstration of a unity of purpose amongst a diversity of impulses.

As the light of our Sun Within, the WILL represents intelligent energy directed toward a definite aim. Like guiding hands extending from the Sun's rays, it is our inner Aten, tending our "Sol-Purpose."

The light of the Sun Within is born of an inner synergy.

It is fed by the burning up of discordant elements in the Individual's psyche. As the energy of this combustion is released, one's various psychological functions become a multi-armed centrifugal force, coordinated to achieve the creation of a superordinate unity.

The Strong WILL

A willed act must contain enough intensity, or "fire," to carry out its purpose. The strength of the WILL can be developed and increased through practice and exercise.

Strength of Will and how to develop it

> Resolution: state, command, or swear an Oath
> with intent to follow through.

Taking an Oath to fulfill a resolution should be done willingly, with precision and a sense of style. Here it's helpful to assume a "sporting attitude" in the best sense of the word, learn to compete with oneself, stretching one's own perceived limits.

Every physical movement is an act of WILL, a command given to the body, and the deliberate repetition of such acts – with attention, effort, and endurance – exercise and invigorate the WILL.

The WILL is to be trained, never exhausted. Resolutely cease working when tired, take wise rest and recreation. A short rest taken in time, at the onset of fatigue, is of greater benefit than a long rest taken after exhaustion.

> An ordered rhythm in our own activities
> generates harmony in our being.

The Art of the Skillful WILL

The WILL can face its match, and often even be overpowered if it consistently puts itself in direct opposition to the other psychological forces, such as the Individual's imagination, emotions, or drives.

Modern psychology has named this tendency "Falsification of Type," a condition in which an Individual moves against the grain of their own innate character to the point of sickness.

If one betrays their inherent disposition long enough this tendency can lead to a very unpleasant condition known as "Prolonged Adaptive Stress Disorder."

Symptoms include: chronic tiredness, lower libido, higher stress, shallow breathing, impotence (romantic or creative), and the list just keeps getting worse. Anyone who has worked for an extended period of time at a job they felt no affinity for has probably felt this to one degree or another.

The contemporary attitude towards applying "willpower" is commonly slanted toward trends of fad dieting and addiction. In this, the frequent mistake is to attempt to force these desired functions into operation by sheer power and direct imposition.

Feeling the long-term impossibility of this task, a more liberal approach then shifts the balance of power wildly in the opposite direction: to abdicate the willed effort entirely, allowing urges, drives, and desires to "happen" without any regulation or consistent direction.

The social and political ramifications of this are evident in every city currently overrun by homeless encampments.

The WILL is capable of achieving its purpose provided it is not only strong but also skillful. The essential function of the skillful WILL is the ability to develop that strategy which is most effective, entailing the greatest economy of effort.

A keynote of strategy is that the most effective approach is seldom the most obvious. Instead, a symphony of indirection that manifests in a sort of surprise flanking maneuver has been the fingerprint of history's greatest strategist.

The role of the WILL can be as a source of direct power or force, or when at our command, its function can stimulate, regulate, and direct other functions and forces in our being so that they're synergistically enhanced through precise alignment with one's predetermined goal.

Will and Love

> In its supremacy, the force of our Daimon is a union of Love and Will.

Our calling is the Love felt for the idealized aspiration embodied in our Grand Vision. The True WILL is the expression of that Love as a desire to serve that ideal, a service which simultaneously drives our consciousness toward a consummate union (or Yoga) with the end goal of its manifestation.

The active development of the WILL, and its expression of Love may also contain some inherently destructive impulses, especially in dealing with the elimination of those obstacles that stand between the WILL and its beloved.

> The weakness of an untempered Will is that it lacks heart.

Love without WILL can make an individual weak, sentimental, over-emotional, and ineffectual. Similarly, problems often arise when a WILL is cold, stern, and even cruel because, taken too far, these qualities represent a lack of Love upon which the WILL depends for its nourishment and renewal.

It's been said that a powerful Love can bear all, and so we incorporate its strength into our philosophy of True WILL.

One of the principal reasons for society's tumultuous history is the lack of love on the part of those who have WILL and the lack of WILL in those who are good and loving. This points to the Individual's urgent need for the integration and unification of Love with WILL.

Love is a great motivator, enticing individuals to overcome great obstacles for its sake. This Love is a natural ally of WILL.

In this, Love helps to solve the problem of "energy." The WILL-er is a directing agent of energy. From the vantage point of the SELF, it is not a compromise between Love and WILL, but a synthesis.

At the heart of the Daimon's influence, and its prompting, is principally a love for oneself. Although the "self" referred to here is something greater than one's personality, it's more a love for the totality of the completed SELF.

Also embedded in the philosophy of True WILL is the recognition that one's WILL is an echo of Universal WILL. This means that added to the equation of "love of Self" is a sort of impersonal love, a love for an idea or ideal.

It has often been an Individual's fascination with an idea, or the beauty of an idea, that has given birth to a WILL whose dedication and self-sacrifice is of the highest order. In other words, a WILL so powerful that it appears to many as an expression of the WILL of God.

Our idea of God represents our *Supreme Value*, or in Jung's words, the Individual's *Supreme Meaning*. It is alignment with this Supreme Meaning that liberates the extraordinary energy capable of producing that sense of awe, wonder, or admiration which men call worship.

> At higher levels, the WILL is directed toward objectives and purposes.

As basic needs are being taken care of, a higher need gradually emerges. Its eminence asserts itself, drawing one toward an ever greater expansion of their consciousness.

The Individual's multiplicity of tendencies, often manifesting as seemingly autonomous and conflicting elements, must be coordinated around an authoritative central intelligence, in other words around their Sun Within.

To this end, the psyche increases the harmonious interaction between the various elements of its nature, like a cosmos moving from its early stages of primal collisions, toward the culmination of an ordered harmony expressed in the Individual as a final fusion into an integrated human being.

In the postmodern era the inherited basis of our capacity for WILL and decisions has been destroyed.

Just when human technological power has grown to monstrous proportions, when God is celebrated as dead, when every supporting pillar of Mankind's existence has been criticized and attacked – exactly at the moment when quality, willful decisions are so necessary, Man ironically finds himself with no real basis for WILL.

Freud cut down the traditional concept of WILL-power in his claims that all motives and behaviors are the result of "unconscious" urges, anxieties, and fears.

This has had the effect of undercutting the Individual's sense of responsibility for their own life. In the view of Freudian psychology we are now unconscious victims of our upbringing, instincts, collective fears, and traumas. Not just our own personal traumas, but also the collective traumas of the past.

The Individual, no longer seen as responsible for their character, comes to believe they are a passive victim of forces they can not control.

Being determined by these unconscious social constructs, or various social factors, the Individual is no longer seen as the driving force of their own destiny, now merely being "driven," or passively riding along in the ox cart of social consensus.

Marx also added to this with his "class war" ideology, lumping Individuals into economic heaps whose state of affairs was determined exclusively by economic matters.

This tendency to see ourselves as the victims of determinism has also been spread by the popular conviction that we are all now helpless in the face of scientific and technological forces such as nuclear weapons and A.I.

The nuclear age played a major role in killing Mankind's faith in its ability to influence what happens to it.

The central "neurosis" of modern man is the undermining of the Individual's experience of responsibility, sapping Mankind's WILL along with its ability to make decisions. This has led to civilized man's experience of inner impotence which has only exacerbated the dilemma of finding real solutions to modern problems.

While we are being constantly reassured that modern man is more powerful and well-off than ever, the average human is plagued with self-doubt about their own decisions, all the while being subtly assured that there is nothing any single person can do to stop the destructive, downward momentum of the boulder which is now heading our way.

The theme is both "God is dead" and the Individual "is not a God," a spiritual crisis that leaves everyone stranded on a sinking ship. We are to be content with the fact that we are all just pawns on a merchants chessboard, a conglomerate of personal information being calculated in a dictatorial algorithm.

God made a form out of chaos, and humans have made chaos out of that form. The postmodern fear is that we can no longer turn that chaos back into form again. To even mention the possibility of an eternal "sacred order" is an act of sedition against contemporary "pop" culture.

Toward whose aims have we progressed since dethroning the ancient King?

"What did we do when we unchained this earth from its Sun?"

- Fredrick Neitzsche

In all these promises of great technological power, a passive role is expected of the Individual, conformity has become the law.

In advertising, education, and health, things are done *to* us.

The transcendentalist ideas of American authors like Emerson and Thoreau, whose sublime song of spirit was that "One is Captain of their own Soul" has been undermined in culture and condemned as a social heresy.

The curious predicament is that the same processes which make modern man so "powerful" are also the same processes being crafted into shackles which render the average person powerless.

We are reassured by Freudian psychology that "will is an illusion anyway" and become caught, as Robert Laing put it, in a "hell of frenetic passivity." This is the obstructed inner impulse of Nietzche's "last man" constantly being re-castrated by the feeling that nothing can be done about anything anyway, so why try…

This is at the heart of "the ironic attitude," the final indignant smirk a fool makes before taking the last step off a cliff… and down into a crevasse that descends into a darkness without end.

People who cannot fill the void with meaningful activities are confronted with an endemic apathy that breeds impotence, addiction, and self-destructive hostility.

> Psychoanalysis was brought into being by the failure of Will.
> – Rollo May

Freud tried to frame the WILL as an implement of repression. He sought to enforce the "vicissitudes of instincts," and the "fate of the repressed libido" as the motive of human activity.

Freud tried to frame the WILL as the devil of the whole system. To his misguided thinking, WILL was claimed to be a negative function of setting resistance and repression into motion.

This marked the moment when the unconscious became heir to the power of WILL.

> "Freud spoke out of and reflected an objectivistic, alienated marketplace culture.

He needed to replace Will because of the requirements of his scientific model, his aim and desire being to make a deterministic science based on the image of nineteenth century natural science. He thus needed a quantitative, cause and effect system: he speaks of his mechanisms as 'hydraulics.'

Will is the capacity to organize one's Self so that movement in a certain direction or toward a certain goal may take place. Wish is the imaginative playing with the possibility of some act or state occurring."

- Rollo May, Will and Love

Ritual as wishing, Routine as WILL-ing

No wish is possible when we first wish it. The concept of "wishing" is what one does when what is desired is something not possible to achieve of one's own power. In contrast, WILL is that affirmation that the end we desire is, in fact, within our own power.

When one's WILL is centralized and synchronized, one experiences an absence of inner conflict, which some will call "flow," a state of consciousness in which one is able to attain their ends almost spontaneously, almost effortlessly.

Healthy Will vs. Unhealthy Will

A healthy WILL defines a definite course of action. It is the response to "a vision" – a clear, unified conception whose coordinate motives are synchronized to be in the right place at the right time in the correct ratio to each other.

An unhealthy Will represents the "obstructed will." This dilemma is characterized by great fatigue or exhaustion.

It is the collective moan of the obstructed Will which is at the heart of the chronic, endemic, psychic state of contemporary society. As the bearer of anxiety, it is the irregular heartbeat of the neurotic personality.

The central problem of WILL is *attention*.

Attention, or intention, is the experience of being firmly seated upon the Throne of TRUE WILL. This is the purpose behind our meditative practices. The exercise of WILL is really an exercise of attention, or the power to remain focused.

In our attention is a connection to belief. Belief and attention share common ground, one whose borders are conterminous with WILL.

WILL begins as the Individual's protest against a world that they never made. Divine Right, or Heaven's Right, is an assertion of one's Self, as co-creator, in the endeavor to remold and reform the world into a renewing image of increasing perfection, onward toward a triumph embodied in the *Holy Grail*.

The WILL and the Royal Art

The Rod of TRUE WILL is *the royal cubit*, the measure or "ruler" which gives meaning to structure – a constructive life whose columns are vertical, straight, and upright.

TRUE WILL is the Individual's essential drive, the essence of all the needs embedded in their nature.

An imperfect or incomplete satisfaction of this WILL results in a stunting of the Individual's essential nature.

Failure to satisfy this WILL brings about the famine of the SPIRIT, the destruction of the possibility of ultimate fulfillment which is the potential harvest of the SELF.

Satisfying this WILL represents the satisfaction of the Individual's deepest needs and the attainment of MAN's highest, most valued ENDS, and thus a life of prosperous well-being (or WILL-being).

This makes it the most important of human endeavors, and thus the foundation of all others.

TRUE WILL is the act of satisfying the deepest needs of consciousness. It is the ultimate endeavor toward which the Individual feels an obligation to succeed. Its exaltation is a concentrated expression of energy as a unity of purpose.

Expressed in the satisfaction of this WILL, is also a desire *to command* the manifestation of things upon which this satisfaction depends: namely love, wealth, health, and conscious fulfillment of various others.

TRUE WILL represents one's growth and development towards these "higher needs." To discover one's TRUE WILL is to discover the Universal WILL, as it relates to oneself.

TRUE WILL represents the "requirements" of consciousness i.e. of the Individual's wholeness.

WILL is the action of SOLAR FORCE, as directed by the Individual.

Sol-Oath / Sol-Conviction

To develop WILL-power, one must cultivate a united purpose in their being, a Sol-Conviction to which they may become committed through a Sol-Oath.

This means taking up the WILL, or Rod-of-Becoming, and committing to its necessary processes.

The ROD is the cross we bear, our WILL.

The length of the Rod, and its measurements, is our "ruler" for measuring and marking the respective stages of development toward one's willed end.

In this measure is our alignment with True WILL, *and* the greater cosmic forces and implications embodied in it. To represent this fact, the Rod also bears the markings of *The Royal Cubit* to symbolize the universal, or transpersonal function of one's highest WILL.

The Rod, as the Royal Cubit, is the measure that accounts for the totality of forces manifest in the Solar System, including: the energy and speed of the Sun's light, the forces of magnetism and gravitation, the circumference of the Earth, and the speed of its rotation; all these and more are contained in the Royal Cubit as expressed in the construction of many ancient temples.

When the personal WILL, or Rod, bears the stamp of the Royal Cubit, it acts as a symbol, calibrating the WILL with those natural laws of the manifest universe which play a decisive role in determining the measure of what is actually possible in one human lifetime.

In this, accepting the existence of human limitation does a great deal to end the anxiety that comes from unrealistic expectations.

The "CUBIT," is the divine measure of the order we build.

It is the ruler by which we calibrate the measure of revelation granted to us in a particular incarnation.

One's WILL must be squared with universal principles if it is to be "true."

If our willed actions were not squared to the measure of the Royal Cubit then they would be out of alignment with universal law and its necessity.

As a result, such a WILL would be delusional, ill-framed, ill-constructed, neither "right" in the squaring of its beams or "true" in the integrity of its supports.

Such a WILL would find itself set against the law of proportion, the Golden Ratio itself, and hence against the order of the cosmos.

This kind of asymmetrical aspiration is doomed, like a leaning column, to become the prey to gravity – just another ill-conceived plan pulled to the ground as an offense to greater cosmic law.

Instead we want our WILL to represent all the Truth, Beauty, Proportion and Magick embodied in the mathematical concept of *the Golden Ratio*.

This is the most mighty foundation upon which to build one's pyramid of consciousness – the square of willed structure amongst the circle of the ALL.

Tools of the Royal Art:

The Rod is: A branch of Wood (often imagined as a branch from the Tree-of-Life). One very useful form is a wooden dowel rod 36"x 1" sanded and inscribed in a balanced way with the dimensions and measurements of the Royal Cubit.

Ritual Practices:

The primary ritual of the Will is that of affirmation, as in the confirmation or fulfilling of an oath. Typically this manifests as: (1) a written script embodying the spirit of the oath, (2) a directive toward an end goal, (3) framed within the constraints of time and (4) crowned by some result that indicates the specific point when the oath will have been fulfilled or the ritual performed to its completion. Define the "Crowning Moment."

Along the way, the oath may include restrictions or limitations of "anti-intentions" – those words, deeds, and thoughts that belong to rites contrary to the stated WILL. This means a disciplined refusal to commit offenses, whether in word, thought or deed, against that which one has affirmed in their oath.

This may include abstaining from "causes" capable of hindering one's desired "effect." In other words, engaging in that which works against the fulfillment of one's WILL, represented in the oath.

CHAPTER THREE

THE HOLY CUP

The Mother of Deeds

Key Words and Phrases: Understanding, Contemplation, Intuitive Insight, Sangreal, Synchronistic Mysteries. Initiation, the Mother of Sovereignty

Ritual: Meditation

Element: Water

Suit in cards: Hearts

In the Tarot: The Cups

Nordic Runes: Perthro, Berkana, Laguz, Isa

Temple Building: Finding Level, Setting the foundation, Blueprints and deeper implications of structural framework

The Cup of the Holy Grail

The CUP is the GRAIL, the Mother of DEEDS.

The Grail is the symbol of what gets one's dopamine neurons firing. It is the ultimate symbol for what unleashes that promise of reward that compels one to seek satisfaction.

As the GRAIL, *it is the prize*, it represents "having it ALL."

THE ALL, is the measure of the ultimate, this means the pursuit of things higher than mere material concerns.

To possess the Grail is to be rich on all levels.

The CUP represents UNDERSTANDING and GNOSIS. It is filled with the BLOOD OF THE SUN.

It is the vessel of solar consciousness.

Filling this Cup represents the collecting of energies toward an ultimate pursuit, a "level up" attainment.

We drink from the CUP when we have trance-formative experiences. Categories of religious experience go here, as well as meditative experiences and altered states including, but not limited to, various forms of intoxication.

The openness required by the CUP is an act of WILL. One must be open to receiving influence from above, from the Sun, from their Daimon.

This is the crossroads of Initiation.

One sign says "this way to candyland" and to this destination aimless fool's are lured. The other sign reads "to the Holy Grail." This is the way of the few.

Candyland allures the many, like insects into a pheromone trap. Its sweet skittles colored road offers empty promises of happiness, a delusional seduction of easy to consume treats.

The other road is *the Royal Road*. It reveals a wide open landscape entered through a set of large stone pylons. Beyond the threshold of this gate marks the first step on a quest for the Holy Grail, that's to say, on a quest to obtain the ultimate expression of whatever one is *called* to do, create, or become.

The Symbolism of the Cup

The Cup has an open top. Its purpose is to receive and dispense. In order to do this a Cup must also possess or hold depth.

In Ritual, the Cup sits upon a level, solid, altar with a lamp above it. Sitting solidly, the liquid inside finds its level and the surface becomes still.

In its stillness, the surface of the liquid reflects the light above.

The light above the altar represents *the eternal Solar God-Force*, while the light reflected upon the surface of the water is the image of *the Sun Within, the face of the Daimon*.

Here one makes their Mind into an image of that Cup, where its surface is level, still, and open only to that which is above – the Solar Force.

As time passes, the babbling surface structure of the Mind's inner thoughts and utterances stills. A previously hidden dimension reveals itself. There, reflecting back from the depth of the waters, is an internal light, an image of the Sun Within.

This awareness of the Cup's power, its hidden depth, its mythic dimension, is also the awareness of a hidden intelligence reflecting its bright face back in the waters of the Individual's unconscious Mind.

Once a person's unconscious Mind atunes with this degree of ritual symbolism the results of meditation become an actual experience instead of something done "hoping" for an experience.

Just like riding a bike, once a person gets it, they get it. Once one achieves this "state" its neurological imprint becomes anchored in their awareness.

Q: What is consciousness aware of in this state?

A: Itself alone, a pure state, silent, and unbounded. A state in which consciousness has become its own object.

No experience is more valuable than this. This is the source of genius. It is unmeasurable, consciousness in its unified state, the true source of natural law.

The Nature of the Cup

The nature of the CUP is containment. It is a vessel.

In its nature is the power of reception and reflection, both aspects of meditative and contemplative states. Contemplation is con-tempulum, meaning *what one does in the temple.*

There is stillness on the water, bringing with it an attitude of royal repose…tranquility…and illumination.

Upon its still waters is the light from above reflected in crystal clear perfection. Perhaps for the first time in their lives the Individual experiences the power of clarified reception, or vision, of inner reality. Upon its glassy, mirror-like surface is a transcendent image reflected from up-above, the SUN WITHIN.

> She, the glow that radiates from eternal light,
> She, the untarnished mirror of God's majesty,
> She, the faithful image of His goodness.
>
> - Wisdom 7:26

What are the aims of meditation?

When the wind of thought is silent and the waves of emotion have ceased, the waters upon the sea find their level and, in this sublime stillness, become like a shining mirror reflecting what is above.

Similarly, in reflective meditation the Mind's eye is directed horizontally, made as still as the water in the cup, and in this reflection it observes the object, or theme of meditation, the Sun Within.

In receptive meditation, the Mind's eye is turned upwards, toward the source, the Sun above, seeking to discover what can be discerned at a higher level than that of ordinary consciousness and of the Mind itself.

In the first stage, the task is to cultivate an inner silence, symbolically stilling the disturbing winds of incessant thought.

Thus stilled, the once fractured image illuminates its wholeness upon the water's surface, no longer distorted. This image, previously a shattered mosaic of confused light, now reveals the face of the superconscious: conveying at once: an intuition, an inspiration, or message, bearing the revelation of a higher stimulus to action.

Meditation involves the elimination of thought processes that have the habit of pulling the mind back down into everything consciousness.

These demanding thoughts often come dressed in the street clothes of personal worries, problems, and internal squabble about things that "need" to be done, or a fretted regurgitation and analysis of events that have already happened.

At first, to keep and maintain this inner silence entails continuous effort.

The western Mind, unaccustomed to this kind of discipline, attempts every conceivable trick, both rational and irrational, including but not limited to hallucination, in order to keep the momentum of thought processes active.

What the Mind is really trying to escape is the inertia of inner peace, which it perceives as boredom and death, knowing instinctively that if a top ceases to spin, it will be toppled. Because the Mind only knows itself by its movements, for the Mind to cease to move is, similarly, the collapse of the momentum of Mind.

Valuing our Mind, and its products above all else, to silence our thinking processes seems to most westerners as undesirable, even a threat to one's very existence.

Cultivating this degree of inner stillness can require, at first, a great deal of time and effort.

In this effort towards stillness, of taking command of one's own thinking processes (rather than being at their constant mercy) is the cultivation of a strength of WILL necessary to receive clear communications from one's Daimon. This meditative state represents the preliminary development of the divine WILL.

It is the development of this skill that lays the foundation for ascending levels of reception and higher communication by which the WILL can be informed, charged and inspired to divine action.

This answers an essential preliminary question: "Why, if the WILL is principally active, do we begin its development by cultivating what seems like a passive, receptive, contemplative state?"

The reason: is that because to do this is unnatural to most modern people, and so the practice of attaining this state subsequently develops the WILL, at once both strengthening the WILL and also laying the groundwork for achieving clear and uninterrupted insight from higher levels of consciousness.

The problem for most "mystical" types is that they tend to think of meditation as an end in itself, and do nothing more, whether they develop the skill or not.

Using a building metaphor, meditation establishes a horizontal line for leveling the foundation upon which we can then proceed to build our enduring structure of consciousness.

The WILL, then, is the perpendicular line as a guide, squaring our work to what is "true."

Perceiving these hidden, but coordinating factors, we will have a level base conjoined with a perfectly upright trajectory. Thus our Pyramid escapes the downward pull of gravity that weakens and collapses imperfect structures.

In this, our supporting actions will be squared with reality. It is quality craftsmanship that will cause our Pyramid to rise with strength from a sure base, and to endure.

The reason some people choose to just make meditation the entire basis of their practice is that once the state is actually achieved, it is highly pleasant.

Coming back from these deep meditative states into the waking world with all its demands, necessities, and duties can feel like coming back from a vacation to return to work.

But here the return to work is really to the service of the inspired WILL.

After initial attainment in meditative practice it no longer requires a great act of WILL to achieve this state, as it did in its preliminary phases.

It becomes so easy, in fact, that it eventually becomes the easiest thing to do, which is the primary indicator of success in meditation.

Here, it's important to avoid letting the passive consume the active. There must be a necessary balance between both.

After a period of great activity, we can return to the meditative state, as a person might recharge a battery. This is the posture of "royal repose," a state of ease that keeps the Individual and their WILL vital.

Meditation requires maintaining a steady, patient attitude of the objective observer for a certain time.

As a strategy to attain eventual silence, persistently repeating a word or phrase in the form of a mantra gives the mind something to occupy it.

Thoughts are then isolated to just ONE thought, in the form of the mantra. Simultaneously, inner dialogue is replaced by this same repetitive phrase. To abandon one thought is easier than to abandon many.

As the mantra is repeated the Individual's breathing becomes rhythmic and consistent, which also has a calming effect upon their psychological state.

During the early stages of developing this skill, sleep and a sense of heaviness sometimes interfere. Sometimes psychic energies, in the form of waking dreams or hallucinations erupt from the unconsciousness.

It's important to note that what we are ultimately looking for here are not hallucinations, waking dreams, or the kaleidoscope of visual tricks and detours concocted by the subconscious mind.

Rather, we're seeking an unusual type of inner dialogue with a previously unknown part of the mind. However, prudence is necessary.

At times "voices" are experienced and "messages" are received, transmitted by the personal or collective unconscious. Some of these messages may be skewed versions of the truth. In the human mind there are some autonomous, unconscious elements that have the power to deceive, dominate and obsess. These elements are enemies posing as friends, devils dressed as angels.

Schizophrenia, mania, neurosis and psychosis are examples of the power of uncontrolled elements operating at a subconscious level. Many people's lives get derailed by unconscious elements. In contemporary society, mental illness is no longer a rare occurrence.

More and more people are suffering from blinding delusion. Fewer and fewer are those guided not by billboards, ads, or political fads, but rather by a deep and powerful sense of inner knowing.

The question to answer is, "How, and in what form, do these 'divine messages' come? In what form are they received?"

Answer: They come as messages or experiences of illumination in the form of an inspired vision, one built from a level base and ascending upright at a 90–degree angle culminating in a capstone of divine completion.

In other words, they come as visions of something so beautiful, so well founded, so implicitly true, and so immaculately conceived that they bear the fingerprint of divinity itself.

This level of illumination may be termed "contact."

This is the experience of being in rapport with the part of one's Mind which Yeat's called "that other Will." It is the experience of an inner contact, an awakening of an innate intelligence along lines previously unknown to oneself, in short, communion with the wisdom of the Inner Initiator, one's Daimon.

Contact with this internal force represents a strong stimulus to action.

From this stimulus often come certain strange and unusual powers. These powers are then explicitly applied in service of the urge aroused to do a given thing, to embark upon a particular activity, or assume certain duties and tasks.

Once a clear awareness of what has been received emerges into consciousness, it's advisable to record this immediately in writing.

Fixing one's experience in written terms can sometimes help one continue receiving as they write. Writing also helps to develop the experience along more conscious lines for greater understanding.

Creative Meditation

There are also various forms of creative meditation incorporated for the purposes of self-creation. During creative meditation we concentrate on mentally constructed images.

Once a mentally constructed image can be held in the mind, and sustained, then it can be modified, transformed, and even regenerated.

When we use a symbol representing our "Sun Within" as this image, then the evolution of this symbol represents an evolution of personality.

This is the Art of applying the creative WILL to the meditative process.

Realization

Realization, in the highest sense, means activating and expressing potentialities residing in the Individual's super-conscious.

This potentiality is represented in the vision of the Sun Within, the direct awareness of the Daimon. Intuiting the relationship between the Sun-above, as it shines down, and the Sun Within as it reflects up from the waters is the first conscious confirmation of their unification. The personal Self, or "I," is an upward aspiring reflection of the Transpersonal Self, or Daimon.

This unity is celebrated in the Solar Mass, or communion, where the Transpersonal Self, or Daimon, is united with the Universal Sun (or the Highest God) in the sacrament of the Holy Cup.

Partaking of this Cup, then, is to become intoxicated by an inspiration that has that descended from the Highest God.

In taking communion with one's inner fire, the connection is made. The spark that lights the torch of the Individual Will has indeed descended from the Sun. In this, Individual WILL becomes an echo, or reflection, of the Universal WILL.

Here we enter the stomping ground of consciousness occupied by prophets, priest-kings and solar heroes. Here we congregate with the highest mystics of all times and places.

Union of Subject and Object

The union of subject and object is when Individuality and Universality are united in a blissful synthetic realization of two becoming one. The sexual parallel will be obvious here.

The WILL is the function most closely in relation to what one considers one's SELF. It is the Individual's experience of the most direct expression of their "I AM."

In the early stages the Individual experiences their WILL, and what Yeat's called "that other WILL," as two separate WILLs.

Revealed later is an intersection of these two converging WILLs upon a single point and in rotation around that point. This often occurs to consciousness in some form of the Solar Cross.

There is both a personal WILL, emanating from what we call "I" and there is a Transpersonal WILL emanating from what we might (as a corollary term) call the "EYE."

In other words, there is the Individual, the Daimon, and the Sun whose solar light descends from one through to the other. In this way, the hands of the Sun's rays of light become the hands of Man.

The inspired words, thoughts and deeds of the Solar Individual come more and more to represent the manifesting life of the Sun's light; with their acts directed upward in the form of a pyramid. In this shape their very existence is built in alignment with the source of life from which their WILL originated.

The Transpersonal WILL (that other WILL) is an expression of the Transpersonal Self (one's Daimon) whose force originates from what might be called the superconscious sphere of the psyche. It is the action of the Daimon which is felt by the personal self, or "I" as "The Call."

This experience has been reported by many Individuals throughout history.

Its experience forms the bedrock not only of every great Individual's sense of destiny but also of almost every religion and every religious experience of Mankind. As such, it has often been recorded as a call from some God-force or higher being in history's holy books.

Accounts from these books often speak of a "call," or dialogue between Man and this "Higher Source." During this intercourse, each alternately invokes and evokes each other.

In some cases the pull from "above" takes the form of an imperative demand. This demanding influence can, at times, be temporarily felt as a sort of persecution.

> The Call is a higher principle…one is "called"
> by their Daimon.

It is through the influence of this principle that prophets, mythic personalities and history's great Individuals (those names who perish not) achieved a transcendence of consciousness which guided them through the storms, battles, and ordeals that act as landmarks on the journey to the divine.

The Universal Will

Does Universal WILL really exist? And if so, what is its relation to Individual WILL? This is a difficult question. First, what if the Universe has no WILL of its own, no organized intelligence guiding the development of life?

If there was not a Universal WILL, then Man would possess something (WILL) not existing in the Universe itself — outside the consciousness of Man. If this is true, then Man's WILL is an exalted reality by virtue of being the singular known existence of conscious intention in the Universe.

However, this would mean that the microcosm would be superior to the macrocosm. Man would possess WILL, direction and intent, but what good would it do upon a rudderless Earth, drifting without direction in a sea of cosmic currents, lost within a Universe with no captain at command?

If neither the Universe nor Man possessed a WILL, then no development would be possible. Either way, the WILL of Man is something not only special, but necessary.

Here we touch upon the age-old question, answered only by revelation: "what is the relation between Man and the ultimate reality — between the Individual Will and the Universal Will?"

To those who haven't had this experience, it is either a theoretic conjecture or a primitive hallucination. By those who have experienced it, this relationship is an affirmed existential reality.

For those who hear the Call of Universal Law "as their own," there becomes an intimate relation between Self and Universe, and its umbilical cord is the WILL.

In the Cup's communion are the unification of the two WILLs as ONE. At this communion, the Individual is no longer merely a mortal man, but a willing participant in the rhythms of Universal Life.

It is this highest level of WILL, in its fusion with Universal WILL that Spinoza called "the willing acceptance of one's destiny."

This is the supreme act of *Amor Fati*, the realization of the highest unrealized need of humanity – the unification of Man's WILL with God's WILL.

Realized in meditation, the Individual, the Daimon and thus the Sun, are in WILL, ONE.

Grand Vision of the Aim or Goal

The chief characteristic of the volitional act is the existence of a purpose to be achieved; the clear vision of an aim, or goal, to be reached.

To command a fully effective WILL we must understand how to WILL a thing completely, without getting lost somewhere along the way.

We must possess the tenacity to successfully cultivate the willed objective from its inception through to its culmination.

So long as the vision or goal remains in the realm of the imagination, or contemplation, it is not yet a WILL in *action*.

First, the aim must be *value* assessed; then it must arouse *motives* which generate the *urge* and the *intention* to achieve it. The word "motive" itself indicates something active, dynamic. Motives are aroused by the *values* that we attach to the goals we seek to attain. Many possible goals exist. We certainly cannot attain them all singley and much less so all at the same time.

A Goal, and a path to it, must be determined.

The Call has been heard, now a WILL must arise to answer it.

Tools of the Royal Art:

The Cup is: the actualization of a superior state of consciousness. From the Cup flows the waters of life and renewal, i.e.. initiation. The attainment of the Holy Cup represents the ultimate quest of life itself.

Ritual Practices:

The Ritual of Gnosis, or Meditation is the primary ritual of The Cup.

At the core of this ritual's mythology is the ritual of sacrifice, or renunciation, during which the aspirant willingly relinquished specific thoughts, words and deeds.

Fundamentally, the performance of the actual ritual of Meditation itself calls for the sacrifice of: extraneous body movement, fidgeting, outside disturbances, forms of distractions, and habitual thinking patterns.

This pattern of sacrifice leads step by step, up the summit of a great pyramid, sacrificing more and more baggage to attain its heights, while simultaneously immersed in a continually growing awareness of the Cup's hidden depths, both descending and ascending in rhythm.

When it comes to sacrifice, the Goddess of the Cup desires blood.

Like Love, which the Cup represents, the Ritual of Gnosis will ultimately ask for a sacrifice of one's own inner monologue so as not to defile its bed-chamber.

At the Cup's High Mass will be the ritual sacrifice of the isolated human personality itself.

From the pierced Heart love flows its life into the Cup.

At the High Mass, the supreme moment finally arrives when all that one has cherished in the form of well-established thinking processes and even the sovereignty of Reason itself is sacrificed as the image of "the Dying God."

The mythos of Communion implies the concepts of regeneration and renewal.

The mythos of the Holy Cup, its dying god image and resurrection narrative, is the feeling of having given everything, only to find it wasn't everything.

Contained in its mythos is the irrational sensation of giving everything and yet still, somehow, receiving more.

This is the principle theme behind many traditions of ancient spiritual practices, and various forms of initiation. Aspirants were frequently stripped of everything but a cloak and rice bowl, or a sword and a shield respective to the orders into which they enlisted.

During initiation's prolonged rituals, aspirants consciously separate themselves from the world around them, sometimes shaving their heads, growing beards or taking on the regalia of a monk or holy person to signify their new pursuit. With concentrated focus, in solemn preparation, these types prepare themselves to own the great battle of life.

In the Ritual of Meditation the sacrifice of thought, both reasoned and unreasoned, is considered the supreme act of faith, affirming by proxy the existence of something greater than or beyond one's own thinking processes or present comprehension, a reality which the Holy Cup itself represents.

Meditation

> Sit still. Sit straight up. Rest your hands on your lap or legs.
>
> Avoid any type of fidgeting.
>
> You can feel the urge to move, but avoid following that urge.
>
> Learn to avoid automatically following every single impulse that your brain and body produce.
>
> Coming back to the breath, again and again, kicks the prefrontal cortex into high gear and quiets the stress and craving centers of your brain.
>
> Thoughts in meditation are like muscle soreness from exercise, it decreases with time.
>
> Meditation requires that a person catch their mind moving away from the goal, and point it back again.
>
> Time and place of ritual meditation is generally considered important. A pilgrimage is the symbolic pursuit of these proper conditions.

Breaking the cycle of distractions

Meditation is not about getting rid of thoughts; it's about learning not to get so lost in them that a person forgets what their goal is.

To feel and adequately respond to the electrical charge of the Daimon/Genius/Higher Self, one needs to strengthen both their systems of self-awareness *and* self-control.

Practical Matters

Meditation has some practical functions so far as health. The breathing practices have benefits in themselves and the calming effect produced by controlled, rhythmic inhalation and exhalation often has the effect of greater mental clarity and lowered stress cortisol levels.

In the west, meditative practices are generally looked upon as passive waste of time because to outer appearances one is generally "just sitting" and not actually doing anything externally productive.

It is specifically this fast from practical concerns that sets in motion the unconscious processes during meditation.

No longer preoccupied with the external world, the Mind's eye turns back on itself and its vision. With no other orientation, the consciousness of Man naturally finds itself illuminated by the Sun Within.

Once an Individual has bathed in this internal light, they are rejuvenated, their WILL is enhanced, their Mind is centered, and their understanding of how cause and effect work in their own inner cosmos is illuminated.

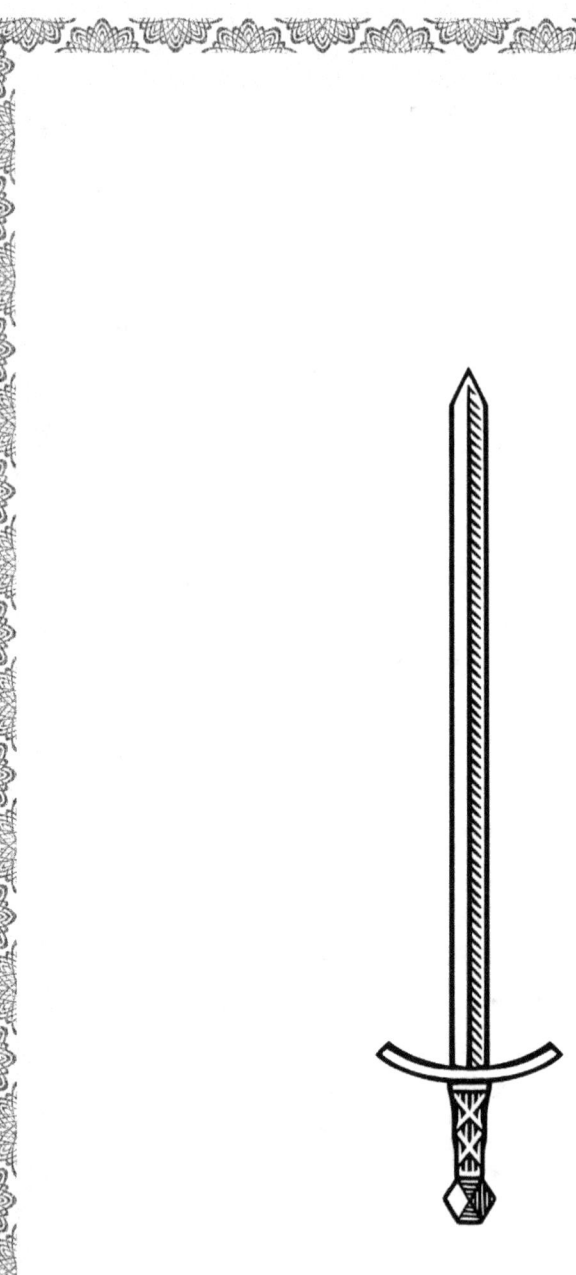

CHAPTER FOUR

THE SWORD

Guardian of Right Action

Key words and phrases: True, Right, Square, Mark, Vigilance, Precision, Judgment, Reason guided by WILL

Ritual: Defining lines, crafting strategies, making objective decisions

Element: Air

Suit in cards: Spades

In the Tarot: The Swords

Nordic Runes: Tiwaz, Kenaz, Gebo, Raido

Temple Building: Angles, Degrees, Squaring Tool, Drawing Blueprints, Analyzing Designs

---

"Great minds have purposes, others have wishes."

- Washington Irving

The powers of the Sword:

>   Intellect (reasoning, objectivity)
>   Discrimination (recognizing a distinction)
>   Demarcation (setting boundaries or limits)

Reason:

Reason is the intellectual faculty that adopts actions to ends. In terms of Sovereignty it involves the establishment of a hierarchy of values and scales of preferences. The Sword of "Reason" is the Son in service of the Father's Will.

>   Its Mother is the CUP which is circumspect,
>   and deep-seeing.

The Mind: a Tool and Weapon

The Sword can be either a tool or a weapon. It can at once be a tool for overcoming problems and a weapon for revealing the chink in the armour of obstacles and opponents.

It is the chief ally of WILL – a pathfinder making a way, cleaving the perceived strength of barriers.

Whereas the WILL is a weapon of unity, concentrating one's forces, the Sword is a weapon of division: dividing to conquer.

The Sword of Reason identifies weak points and strong points. Its blade cleaves problems, revealing the smooth grain of their defeatable parts.

The sharp edge of Reason exposes the vulnerability of seemingly invulnerable monsters.

By virtue of supreme focus, its discriminating point can drive deep into the exact position that causes imposing castle walls to crumble. "Aim the catapult right here, at this exact point," says the General, pointing with the Sword.

The Sword is double-edged, the same weapon is also a tool, versatile and adaptive to almost any call.

With one quick turn, the point of that same assaulting insight can turn its articulation in the opposing direction, describing in detail how a stone must be cut to build a castle that would stand through any attack.

Our Sword is a weapon of defense, whose inscription is etched with a phrase concisely articulating whatever we consider: "A sound value to be zealously guarded."

> By our Sword we cut away contrary ideas.
> This is the power of "No."

These means keeping a sharp discriminatory edge on the blade. By the blade of the Sword our work is kept pure, severing the "devil's tongue."

Here, fine scrutiny is justice.

With the razor's edge of discernment to the throat of delusion, the Sword practices constant discrimination about what really applies to our purpose and what does not.

Upon the blade of the Sword we slay that which leads us astray through idle curiosity about things which do not serve our main purpose in life.

The Sword is the guardian of one's perception, an instrument of DEVOTION, the defender of our ASPIRATION.

A vigilant mind is one with a balanced edge, razor-sharp on both sides.

Upon the blade of this Sword one defends their freedom from emotion and obsession. The Sword guides our actions, severing impulsive, fanatical conclusions.
In this respect, the Sword is the guardian of the way, purifying our kingdom and ourselves of anything that attempts to weaken and sabotage our good work.

Not only must the Sword be kept sharp, but also wielded firmly, with enough confidence and enough heart to make hard decisions with boldness.

> "It is a very bad thing to cut off a person's head half-heartedly."
>
> – Alan Watts, lecture on Bushido

Implicitly, taking up the Sword suggests boldness and action, words which themselves assume the bearer also possesses the courage to face necessary consequences with heart.

Something will be sacrificed in every encounter with a Sword. That's its nature.

The word "Decide" ends in "cide" whose latin meaning is "an act of killing,"
Same as homicide and pesticide.
To decide is to kill an option.
To decide is not "to Choose."
To choose implies a wholehearted, singularly aimed choice.
If we can not choose then we must decide.
To choose requires a higher order of love.
To decide is the cold appraisal of two or more options, neither of which are "first choice."

If we are considering more than one option, then it's implicit that neither leads directly to our beloved, or that each option has some unpleasant sacrifice attached.

This is where we are forced to decide. Out comes the Sword and heads will roll.

First choice is the most cherished by WILL, as it's the most simple and direct route to anything.

Without first choice, WILL governs by decimation, eliminating options from the lowest to the highest like a woodcutter trimming up branches on a tree until only one branch remains.

Decide: "to kill other options"

There are usually a number of goals which we feel an urge to pursue. But it is not possible or practical to pursue all of them.

We must choose the one we most prefer, and deciding to pursue this one means also renouncing and postponing others.

The objective of every deliberation is to lead to the best possible decision.

The Sword covers the dimension of the Mind and analytics which implies the thinking process. Hard thought, like the hard swinging of a Sword can be uncomfortable and tiring; it demands concentration, and this requires a persistent use of the WILL.

Moreover, the reasoned outcome of such thinking may unpleasantly conflict with some of our lower inclinations and drives. To avoid the trap of paralysis by over analysis, and the burnout often associated with this kind of over thinking, it's best to treat the Mind as one would any cutting tool, keeping it sharp and making the cutting motion as smooth, swift and decisive as possible. The fool hacks and hacks at a problem, never seeming to be able to make it through. The master makes a swift decisive cut along a single line.

Keep in mind that to decide is not to choose, it's to slay all unworthy options until only one remains. The last one standing is the most worthy.

All too often, learning to think properly is confused with the memorization of facts.

Chronic intellectuals frequently suffer social fractures from the terrific mental gymnastics they perform to prove a point to themselves and others.

In this regard, proper use of the mind means efficient action, clean cut appraisals and deft mental maneuvering instead of complex formulas.

There is no need to go waving around an oversized Sword to display our intellectual superiority where a quick striking dagger of pointed wit is more effective.

Two lines of poetry can sometimes convey an idea more thoroughly and deeply than an entire volume of fact and theory.

The Cup of Understanding is the Mother of Reason, and part of the inheritance gifted by this descent is the Mind's innate awareness that, as often as not, deeper truths are not the product of reasoning, they're intuitive. Sometimes they can be almost impossible to communicate in anything other than poetic language.

Like the sword-carrying samurai, the way of the life-giving sword first means learning how to reflect and meditate. In mastering the elements within oneself there is a hierarchy of authority. First we drink from the Cup, then we grasp the Sword.

Decision: A matter of sacrifice

To decide implies to prefer one option above others. This necessarily demands the sacrifice of others. To choose means first and foremost to say "no" to the least worthy options offered to us.

One by one we eliminate the others, relinquishing their viable status. The death of lesser options frees their hold on our attention and liberates the life contained in them to be poured into the Cup.

In spiritual matters this is often framed as renunciation and sacrifice. One connection of the relationship between WILL and Reason is that the volitional act requires the subordination of lesser aims and impulses. This is known as the power of inhibition.

Reason guides and makes final decisions against those subordinate drives, aims, impulses, and tendencies that are in competition with one's chosen aim, their WILL.

This is handled very differently from postmodern therapy which exalts vulnerability and declarations of trauma and frames emotional discipline as repression.

Willed inhibition means resolutely abstaining from an impulse or tendency for the purposes of deciding how best to deal with it.

We may practice willed inhibition over certain harmful impulses or emotions, holding them back from expression in order to first examine or analyze them.

Once the vetting process is complete we can redirect impulses and emotions, transmute them, or even allow for their expression at a more appropriate time or in a more appropriate way.

The act of decision, making your mark

The act of decision has its prelude in deliberation. We consider the options presented to us, choose from among them, and then make a consequent decision. In the analogy of the stonemason, we measure, we mark, then we cut.

> Our final decision is then confirmed by affirmation.

We draw a line and then commit to cutting exactly on that line. To stay on this line represents the formal structure of "an oath."

A committed decision is one that does not stray from its chosen line.

It says, "this…right here…this is the line…this is where the stone must be cut if the resulting block is to be true and square."

Once the block is hewn true, it is then ready for the Temple. It becomes another master block in the building of the Temple of the Anthropocosmos, the reflective consciousness in Man.

To build the Temple, a careful elaboration of a plan or program is needed.

This implies strategy.

Reasoned decision making means eliminating options, then selecting the best. It also means a consideration and selection of the various means of executing one's plans and coordinating its phases of development: estimating circumstances, conditions and existing possibilities while also considering factors of time.

Reason guided by WILL

Finally, when it comes to the direction of execution, we return to the WILL.

When we talk about our "purpose" we are talking about our WILL to reach a goal we regard as valuable. This is our motive, our call to action. A motive is only a motive if it possesses the energy of movement.

The WILL at first calls up the various functions needed for its purpose. It then gives them definite commands, instructions, and directions.

This direction must also include constant supervision of the WILL's execution. The Individual must supervise these actions, watching their development and seeing that they remain on the right course.

Here use of the Sword entails a decided subordination of the various means to develop these plans in a given direction. At times this may require resolving and refining the underlying purpose behind our WILL as our plans evolve through constant adaptation to changing conditions and circumstances.

To advance the process, the WILL should make skillful use of all psychological, physical and spiritual energies existing in the Individual's character.

These include one's thinking and imagination, perceptions and intuition, feelings and impulses, as well as any physical gifts one may possess.

So, where do the images for these plans and the strong motives that fuel them come from?

Sometimes a motive appears as an ideal on the borders of consciousness, not yet clearly defined, but prompting the Individual's curiosity by its prospective value.

Sometimes the ultimate value of a new idea is unclear, yet later one comes to understand its connection to their WILL.

The mysterious nature of True WILL is constantly revealing the unconscious intelligence of its design. Unknown to the Individual, these new ideas may be an essential puzzle piece in the aim or goal the WILL expresses.

At times the WILL's vision comes as an intuitive flash, like lightning illuminating the valued goal. Charged with life, an inspired idea can arouse dead motives to life through a powerful urge towards the task's actualization.

The magic of these flashes is that, electrified by their inspiring forms, we are more apt to feel that our life has a purpose, one confirmed by higher powers whose gift was the idea. With this conviction firm, the idea's purpose and its meaning are understood to be both valuable and good.

The good and bad of a sharp Sword:

> Good intentions, bad consequences. There is a popular saying that "the road to hell is paved with good intentions."

This refers to the bad consequences that have often followed acts committed with the best intentions… but with little wisdom.

There are many today whose terms of "right" or "wrong" are still caught in the trap of medieval virtue, framing each decision as a challenge in moral terms.

Quality decisions are about quality results more than they are measures of moral worth.

A strange law of human psychology demonstrates how moral compensation operates. Striving to be good in one area of life subconsciously gives us permission to be bad in some other area.

An act of charity gives us permission to cheat somewhere else, while being excessively stingy at one moment might stimulate our unconscious compensatory reflex to be excessively generous at another.

In this way one unjust, unbalanced act leads to another, the water sloshes around the boat, and instead of just holding firm to the rudder a person deviates in wide arcs left and right overcompensating for overcompensating.

For better self-control, forget the ever changing pantheon of moral virtues, and focus instead on central objectives and core values. Through our core values we identify ourselves with our goal, rather than the moral halo of supposed virtue. Let history judge our motives from the vantage point of hindsight centuries from now.

Upon the blade of the Sword one begins to steel themselves against the struggles and conflicts of one's own times. This is both a struggle against one's external enemies, and a mirror of those characteristics one is attempting to purge from oneself.

In the Bhagavad Gita there is *kshatriya* – one who gives protection from harm and is specially trained for challenging and killing. A kshatriya fights because he knows that it is the reason for his existence, his *dharma*.

In this there is no selfish desire or attempt to bring about some temporary political gain. He fights to defend the principles of his religion and his community knowing that if he carries out his duty, regardless of victory, defeat or even his personal safety, he is destined to attain the highest spiritual platform.

What we seek are not rigidly moral acts, but rather acts that are true, and squarely aligned with our purpose. The truth of a particular block depends on what purpose it serves in building the Temple.

Indecision:

> "This is the tragedy of a Man who could not make up his mind…"
> - Lawrence Olivier's opening to Hamlet, 1948

Indecision is often the result of conflicts between our unconscious and conscious motives. Lacking the certainty of internal congruence a person fears making a mistake…and assuming responsibility for its consequence.

One must develop the courage to make mistakes. To decide is inevitable, because either way, even not deciding is itself a decision.

Indecisiveness can sometimes come from a feeling of uncertainty about minor choices of no real importance. Matters like these can easily be decided by the flip of a coin.

Some mentally ridgid people believe they're strong willed when they are merely stubborn. Some people believe they are decisive when they really just restrict their field of vision to a very limited selection, they choose between Folgers and Maxwell House and they make the same choice every week.

For some people, an obstinate pride prevents them from recognizing that their builder's square has become warped. One may deceive oneself, but never gravity. Eventually the passage of time will reveal those blocks were too hastily hewn to bear the weight of the Temple's longed-for pediment.

Others are so changeable that they hold to nothing, seeing imagined potential in every alternative direction, a new ambition at every potential crossroad. Tomorrow they may go back to school to be a banker, a lawyer, a doctor, or an actor.

Change is indeed a part of life, but so is eternity. There are many unchanging laws which govern life. When we tap into True WILL we are tapping into something of the eternal in our nature.

Practicing judgment, swinging the Sword

The SWORD represents analysis, an unemotional, mathematical approach to problem solving.

Judgment begins with knowing yourself, your abilities and biases. Then it extends to knowing other Individuals.

> The Sword is for cutting away resistance, that which saps our willpower.

The Sword cuts away excess baggage. It streamlines our efforts, eliminating drag, trimming away "fat," and cutting threads of unnecessary entanglements that might squander our energies. (Useless talks, purposeless work, futile concerns, ungrounded fantasies, i.e. that which is not our business.) The Sword circumscribes the jurisdiction of our agency.

Failure by fault of insufficient WILL is sometimes due to the tax imposed by uneconomical actions.

A tired, burdened mind is not as sharp as a mind charged with the high morale that comes from advancing great distances with minimal sacrifice.

Strategy: making decisions, producing effects

Strategy involves the ability to foresee cause and effect in the clearest possible light.

> Actions are causes which lead to effects.

Causes may be singular but effects rarely, if ever, are. Like the proverbial stone cast into a lake, the ripples of our actions echo out into eternity, their subtle influence touching distant shores we may not even see.

In our actions are ripples and counter ripples, immediate consequences and long-term ones.

Sometimes the first can turn out different from the last, even becoming its opposite. Immediate gratification may have harmful effects later.

In the training of one's decision making skill, it is best to begin by making decisions about matters of little or no importance, taking one street in preference to another, or similarly, when in a restaurant by deciding on one dish above another.

> Preference implies the elimination of alternatives.

The choice between the past and future

Many old forms do not work anymore. Old ways of life prove increasingly inadequate to meet present needs. On the other hand, the new is not to be chosen in a hurry without discernment. At present we are witnessing violent, excessive, and ill-considered attempts to change everything at once. The wisdom here says we should not abandon established ways before testing new ones.

The Holy Grail and the Sword:
Super-conscious decision-making

Superior decisions often originate via superconscious intuition in the form of illuminations, inspirations, and instinctual urges to action from the Higher or Transpersonal Self.

Often, the origin of these intuitions are uncertain. At times they may even inspire the Individual to undertake actions involving sacrifice and risk.

Do these uncomfortable promptings to act really come from the exalted level of the superconscious? Or are they mere reactions to external influences?

We are continually subject to influences of every kind and source, so being able to distinguish intuition from impulse is imperative.

Firm self-control is needed to avoid excessive emotional reactions that might draw one into taking action too quickly.

The opposite mistake is to excessively criticize the source of one's inspiration, producing doubts and confusion about its validity.

In many cases that original, intuitive flash was right.

Spontaneous inspirations and intuitions activate our superconscious linking it to our conscious personality.

VOCABULARY

A Right Decision

A decision represents a straight cut along an exact line.

> It represents the workings of a Mind squared by Reason.

As such, welding the Sword implies an upright psychological integrity.
This means a level headed approach to problems, never allowing oneself to get carried away by any emotion.
With the Sword we draw an acute distinction between falsehood and truth, with a discriminating eye we seperate brass from gold.

THE SQUARE:

Right thinking, "Squaring" our Reason against TRUE WILL.

Righteousness: the upright, guiding cosmic law or order inherent in the Individual's eternal reality (Dharma).

TRUE:

Firm, solid, steadfast.

Having or characterized by good faith.

Truism – self-evident truth.

RIGHT: Just, good, fitting, straight, not bent, direct, erect. To move in a straight line. Also to rule, to lead straight, to put right – righteous, wise.

RIGHTEOUS: Wise, way, manner – genuine, excellent.

HONE: Old English *Han* "a stone, rock," (boundary stone).

HONEST: Dealing fairly, truthful. From Latin *Honestus* - "Honorable, respected, regarded with honor, deserving honor."

WRITE: Old English *Writan* – "To score, outline, draw the figure of, to scratch, sketch, draw."

RITE: Latin *Ritus* "Religious observance or ceremony, custom." From 'Re' Proto-Indo-European root 'Re' – "To reason, count."

REASON: Intellectual faculty that adopts actions to ends.

RULE: Norman *Reule* - "Rule, custom, religious order." Latin *Regula* "straight stick, bar, ruler" - a pattern, a model. *Regere* - "to rule, straighten, guide." *Reg* Proto-Indo-European - "move in a straight line - to direct in a straight line - mark with lines (write, sketch, scratch) - to lead." Legal sense: to establish a decision.

Square: Tool for measuring right angles – "to square, make square - to set in order, complete." Proto–Indo–European *kwetwer* – four – a number multiplied by itself. French *Escarrer* – "to cut square - to regulate according to a standard." Square – fairly, honest – direct in line.

Truth – the ability to understand the difference between the real and unreal.

Justice

> A logical, well-ordered mindset is necessary to dispense fair Justice.

The Sword points upwards – expressing a firm and final decision. The double edged blade signifies that our actions always carry consequences.

The Sword is the weapon to choose when one needs to make an important choice with the potential for long-term repercussions. In this regard, the Sword implies a degree of insight into the impact one's decisions may have on the well-being of oneself and others.

When commanding the power of judgment, represented by the Sword, be ready to stand by your decisions. As Sovereign, *you will* be held to account for the choices you make.

Here it's important to ask, "Do I stand by my decisions and accept the consequences of my actions?"

Hewing stones: *Becoming a creator of what is right and true*

> The effort to support a "Right" decision is called courage.

REASON is the thoughtful builder, hewing square stones true to form.

If the construction of what we build is guided by the "True Square" of Reason, then what we build will be strong.

In building the Temple of Self, Man's spiritual task becomes like that of the stonemason.

Setting to work, guided by the vision of a perfect idea, a light shines upon the mind of Man, illuminating the blueprint of the Holy Temple.

In accord with the plans of this blueprint, Man seeks to hew the shape of a divine image from the rigid bonds of matter, to see the perfect lines of each building block contained in the rough quarry stone. With chisel and hammer, the spirit in Man sets this divine image free from its bond to an imperfect form.

WILL is the energy to do a thing, right action is the distinct mark a master stonemason makes on the quarry stone, saying: "This is the mark, this far, but no farther."

Man sets to the task of completing the Great Work. In developing this skill, Man learns to rule over the elements of his own nature.

In doing so, Man becomes a *Self-Ruler*.

Man the measure of all things becomes the measurer.

The measure of Man's True WILL becomes the Royal Cubit by which the Temple will be built.

Man as both Master architect and devoted stonemason, measures the material, marks the lines, and cuts each stone in accord with a divine blueprint, raising each block in accord with a higher law whose ultimate reason is hidden in the intricate design of some inconceivably great, cosmic plan.

Guided by the spirit of the Daimon, Man's hands become the builder of the Temple, the creator of the body of a deity, a new image of God that reflects the Anthropocosmos.

"Every moment I shape my destiny with a chisel.
I am a carpenter of my own soul."

— Rumi

Tools of the Royal Art: *The Sword is a double edged cutting instrument, the more balanced in its handling, the better. It ends in a sharpened point, on its blade is etched the inscription of a value zealously guarded.*

Ritual Practices:

The Principle Ritual of the Sword involves concentrating one's moving attention on a single thought, or theme of thoughts and ideas, for the purpose of constructing forms that possess a central point, or motive, and are built upon firm foundations of well established reason.

The Sword and its craft is the object of meditation here. Rituals often include: drawing lines, establishing boundaries, making decisions, calculating numbers, estimating balances, sketching of plans, studying of maps, and the development of strategies.

Likewise, the Sword is the ancient symbol for 'official implementation of action,' as in the phrase: "Drawing one's Sword."

Ritualistically keeping one's blade sharp is, of course, of vital concern. Anything that dulls reaction or lowers sensory and mental acuity dulls Man's powers of Reason. This is the counterbalance between the Sword and the Cup.

Meditation clarifies the Mind of distracting influences, so that Reason's Sword can be wielded with absolute clarity, with one-pointed precision.

At the same time, the Cup holds wine, which is an intoxicant that loosens the bonds of Reason.

Taken to one extreme, the castles built by Reason take on the appearance of prisons, reason searches for reason as a way to validate its own existence. Reason searches for reason in a search for God's reason and is traumatized to find that God's reason is beyond reason.

For Reason, the search for God ends in a baffled state of nothingness. The Mind's quest for God becomes just a confused spiritual runaround with its search pointing both everywhere and nowhere at the same time.

At the other extreme is the potent, inebriating wine in the Holy Cup.
One receptive draught from that Holy Cup and God is revealed to Man.
One drop more from that Cup, beyond the Individual's tolerance, and the same wine consequently possesses the power to break the seal on Reason's gates and swing their consciousness out over the horrors of the abyss of chaos.

With reason's gates ripped from their hinges, the Individual will have no choice but to cross that abyss, prepared or unprepared.

Practical Matters:

Mathematical knowledge can be either abstract or practical, numbers bridge the gap from the irrational to the rational.

The Practical factor of the Sword, and its key strength, is division.

Cutting reality down to a fraction of a fraction of a decimal point, its judgment is exacting. It casts the line that is the practical jurisdiction of its power. It knows what 2% more must go from the nose of a statue to give it the greatest proportion of beauty.

As the Mind, the Sword is a practical problem solver, chunking down problems into manageable parts and then identifying the precise point where the scales of power pivot.

In terms of practical training, the Mind is exercised in the game of chess, in solving problems of math, in constructing anything, buildings, ideas, sentences, paragraphs, pages, and chapters of books. Each reason must conceive of how disparate parts can be welded together with logical connections, and harmonized toward a given end and purpose.

If the Temple is to be a house of wisdom it must first possess a sure foundation and strong, upright columns.

Meditation lays the foundation. The columns ascend through acts of WILL.

To build something, a house or a life, is to solve the question, "Where will the horizontal and vertical axis meet?" This is where we find if the construction of an idea, thought, or argument is "true."

Neurology:

It is good to do things that are neurologically new. At the same time, having some well established rituals is necessary to give one's inner neurological order a structure, and to set in motion a daily rhythm and momentum guided through carefully selected habits.

Here the Sword is used to cut away those strings that connect a person to dead situations, severing any problematic sentimentality to old centers of power which no longer possess an active current of viability.

To reflect the wisdom in sacrificing what is no longer viable, is a saying attributed to the spirit of Freyja, Norse goddess of Love and War, "If you can't lay them, slay them."

Likewise, to fully dedicate oneself to the ritual of WILL, to the legacy of character and destiny, is to know that if one finds themselves unwittingly engaged to a destination that they can't truly *Love and Will*, then it can have no real, long-term value. It is but another sacrifice to be laid upon the altar, an offering dedicated to one's chosen horizon – that place where the Sun reflects on the stoic stillness of eternal waters.

CHAPTER FIVE

THE PANTACLE COIN

Art is the birth of Reality

Key Words: Wealth, Economics, Five-Senses, Cause and effect, Physicality, Generation, Process of building and creating

The Ritual: Producing Bread and Thread, Economics of Purposeful Action

Element: Earth

Suit in Cards: Diamonds

In the Tarot: The Pentacles

Nordic Runes: Fehu, Ingwaz, Nauthiz, Jera

Temple Building: The Stone and the Block, the Pulleys and Ropes, the backs of the workers and the grain that feeds them

---

"Life is a questing after Value."
                                                    - Manly P. Hall

---

The Bread of Life, the Medium of Art

The Pantacle is the practical principle of Spiritual Power.

The PANTACLE COIN is the Material of Earth, one's Resources (WEALTH), one's Physical body, and all the material elements of one's Environment, including time and its products: Causality (Cause and Effect) and the intentional direction of causality by the WILL.

The Pantacle, in this way, connects to "Stragenomics," or the fusion of strategy (limited aims toward limited means) with the science of wealth, Economics (the art of managing a household).

It then adds to this dough the virtues of: (investment) wise use of what we're given and (industriousness) producing goods or effects that result in earnings. By this magick, the Pantacle transforms stale crust into fresh loaves of bread.

Blessed with the Pantacle's effective force, elements of the physical world will become more responsive to one's command and more receptive to one's stamp, returning to your hand, from copper, to silver, to gold, a profit instead of a loss.

The Barns and granaries of your land will be full. Youth will be retained for longer and foolish accidents avoided. Foresight will take the place of hindsight and profits will be earned.

Spells in this element are talismanic. The most potent talismans are those of multiplication, the effect of this being a vigorous growth of numbers.

Masters of the material Craft

Masters use their craft, rather than being used by it.

Masters of the craft know how to maximize the quantity of resources available to them and leverage it toward the greatest possible satisfaction of their wants and needs within the amount of time allotted.

The Material Craft is primarily concerned with magnifying and multiplying the effects of a cause.

The Pantacle's magical equation is:
(A) = minimum valued cause **X** maximum valued effect

The Pantacle as the medium of Art

The PANTACLE is the MEDIUM, upon and through which we work. For the painter it is the canvas. For the writer it is the page. For the sculptor it is the rough block of stone. For the stone lifter, it is their body.

The PANTACLE COIN represents the science of economics. It is the science of ENDS AND MEANS.

For Mankind, the Pantacle's Coin is meant to be a means of exchange, one in which the only wise exchange is that of leveraging material wealth to cultivate one's branch of being and its fruit. There are things more valuable than money and the chief of those is the Crown of Sovereignty.

In this pursuit of ends and means many have been deceived. In their pursuit of means with no higher end, the pursuit of means became an end in itself. They seek the Coin but not the Crown. The Coin is not the CROWN.

The Pantacle as Food

> The Pantacle is the substance of Earth, the flesh of the World.

Everything is food. Food makes the day possible. Mankind goes about its day, shedding and reforming both mind and body, ingesting and excreting.

In both mind and body, what we ingest becomes us.

Food, sound, vibrations, architectural proportions, unions of forms and colors, harmonies and rhythms of music and all the ideas which we come in contact with are a sort of food, and this is implied in the Pantacle.

The Pantacle represents the food of holy communion which is all the karma: the sights, the sounds, the taste and smells, the sensations and all that life has called us into incarnation to experience – all of this is in the Pantacle.

All is absorbed mechanically, through the stomach, mind and senses.

That which we consume becomes us. In food, in thought, in sense, in experience, all the content of our lives is the food of the Pantacle.

Like food, it is often eaten and forgotten, without real attention being paid to all the processes involved for the Pantacle to come to life, for the complex processes of Earth to continue, for seed to become bread, for thoughts to become books, for coins to keep circulating uninterrupted from generation to generation.

Upon Earth's wheel of changing seasons, life dies and renews itself in turn, bound like Christo to a spinning X.

"In the sweat of thy face shalt thou eat bread, till thou return unto the ground, for out of it wast thou taken: for dust thou art, and unto dust shalt thou return."

The Pantacle is the bread we eat in the communion of sweat and toil. The Pantacle is the ground of material reality.

The Law of Necessity

> "Thorns and thistles shall it bring forth to thee...in toil shall it be cultivated... by the sweat of thy face..."

Like the rune Nauthiz, the Pantacle represents the law of necessity. It is the labor of sewing together fig leaves to clothe our nakedness. It is the yoke and spindle upon which Mankind earns its bread and weaves its thread. It is the necessary labor of life in the light of the Sun, whose shadowside is misery and poverty. Either we earn our bread and weave our thread or we go without, cold and a-hungered.

Everything that the five senses can experience is the flesh of the Pantacle.

In Eden, it is said that after eating the forbidden fruit mankind was given "coats of skin" by the Lord – the physical body given to each spirit at its incarnation.

Birth into this world is the expulsion from the womb of Eden. We are born naked, no longer having our needs immediately met by Eden's umbilical cord. From the state of floating buoyancy we descend through Eden's exit gate and into a world whose oppressive gravity we immediately feel.

Birth brings us down flat onto fleshy backs, clothed now in the same reality as the forbidden fruit, all senses are struck by an inrushing of sights, sounds, smells, tastes, and physical sensations both pleasant and unpleasant, alluring and frightful, good and evil.

The physical world is the substance of the fruit, having tasted of the fruit of that tree *we become its fruit*, both its servant and its product.

The fruit cast a potent spell: toward *its* ends we labor.

As humans we shape the substance of life. From its substance bodies are made. From its substance we erect the Temple of Man.

> "A Man is a God in ruins."
> - Ralph Waldo Emerson

The Pantacle is the substance of the Anthropocosmos. The Earth is ever changing. It is the substance that is always being formed, remembering what was and being redefined into what is.

Some spiritual teachers have advocated the destruction of the Pantacle. To escape its bonds has become their primary directive. They have refused the toil and chose instead to sit idle under the Bodhi Tree.

They have refused its bread as a means of spiritual purity and have allowed their bodies to become emaciated.

They have condemned the World itself as evil, and have put all the eggs of their hope into the basket of a world beyond. They have eaten the fruit of good and evil and tasted only evil.

Many have taken up the task of forming the Pantacle, only to despair, their monuments crumble, their empires perish, their wives betray them. And so they take the path of the ascetic. They deny the devil's offer to turn stones into loaves of bread, choosing instead to beg for bowls of rice, and to that end, go crucified upon the rack of unworldliness.

In their hunger they ask, "Where is Heaven?" To which the wise swami replies, "an empty stomach is no good for religion."

In our pursuit of a higher calling we face the necessity of the World. No matter how much we may wish to forego the toil of existence, it is there. Turning plowshares into swords, then after the war, swords back into plowshares is a lot of work.

The money changers at the Temple demand a coin before entry and so many, initially, go about accumulating coins to pay that tax.

In that toil, the Temple is forgotten. They descend from being Men to mere merchants. This is the web of necessity from whose strings many a Man has been hung. This is the Pantacle, the complex situation called cause and effect that is forever changing and shaping the terrain of earthly life.

So what then to do with our time and energy?

What will become our good work? Toward what noble end shall we labor?

The Price

> It's not what a Man is that counts now, it's what he's worth by the hour.
> - Manly P. Hall

The value of a thing is determined by the degree to which the means of attaining it are limited. This is true of all resources, what is free and unlimited goes unappreciated no matter how dependent on it we are.

The value of a thing is the price we pay for it.

The price of birth is death.

The price of incarnation is that mankind must pay the debt on its wants and needs.

The debt to heaven is paid by the blood in the Cup, the debt to incarnation is paid by the Coin. This means that Man's earthly life is largely a pursuit of resources to pay the debt on its wants and needs.

A resource is that which is valued by Mankind as a means of satisfying these wants and needs.

So... we enter into the world of economics. In this we are seemingly only speaking of hard assets and yet by economics we mean more than just material goods.

The purpose of transforming bread into THE BODY OF GOD is that it turns a common, every day, material substance into an "immaterial horde" – that is: the treasure of worthwhile experience.

Man's toil in the garden is by "the sweat of his face," a representation of Mankind's endless search for ways to satisfy its wants and needs.

Immediately upon exiting the bountiful paradise of Eden, mankind sought to increase its production of valued goods.

Abel tended his sheep, Cain became a tiller of the Earth.

In an attempt to increase his available supply of heaven's goodwill, and thereby increase the production of his labor, Man invented a magical recipe: sacrifice to God.

"And in process of time it came to pass, that Cain brought fruit of the ground an offering to the Lord.

And Abel, he also brought of the firstlings of his flock and the fat thereof. And the Lord had respect unto Abel and to his offering.

But unto Cain and his offering he had not respect. And Cain was very wroth, and his countenance fell." - Genesis 4:3-5

This is history's first recorded value judgment, not surprising that it came from God. The decree was thus, the value of a sacrifice is not in the quantity of fibrous pulp offered, but in the quality of precious blood split.

In response, Cain was inspired to spill the blood of his brother.

One drop of blood is worth more than a bushel of cabbages.

Value Judgements: The Pantacle and the Sword

One flake of gold stands out from an entire pan of silt and it is in Man's nature to be able to notice the difference.

The Earth is a composite of materials. Although no part of the whole can be dispensed with, certain things at certain times have a greater value than others.

The scale of value represents the satisfaction, utility, contentment, or "happiness" that a resource can procure.

In the Royal Art, the Pantacle represents our earthly labor as the work of alchemy: turning shit into sugar, shaping rough quarry stones into symmetrically hewed blocks, transforming lead into gold.

Even in the most common sense, that same aim is the point behind all purposeful action. It's an attempt to exchange a less satisfactory state of affairs for a more satisfactory one.

As a result, Mankind is constantly on the pursuit of the means to attain valued ends, to increase its state of satisfaction, contentment and happiness.

Time:

> "I'll lose a man, but never a moment.
> Space we can recover, lost time never."
>
> — Napoleon

All human life takes place in time. A Man's time is always scarce. Man is not immortal. Man's time on Earth is limited. Time is a factor omnipresent in all human action. Time is also the means that Man must use to arrive at his willed ends. Time is always scarce. It is the scarcest resource. The sooner an end can be attained, the better. Man prefers his willed ends to be achieved in the shortest possible time.

Time is scarce for Man only because whichever ends he chooses to satisfy, there are others that must remain unsatisfied. The necessity of choice among ends arises. He must choose. One end can be satisfied, but the others must go unfulfilled. This is the law of sacrifice.

Action takes place by choosing which ends shall be satisfied by the employment of Man's means.

The work of life is aspiring to a higher state. Man labors toward the completion of the pyramid of consciousness, toward the building of the Temple of Man.

In building that Temple, Mankind's interest is to secure means that will satisfy its wants for a longer period of time…ideally for eternity.

In erecting this Temple, one's actions involve the employment of scarce means (time, money, and energy) to the attainment of Man's most valued ends (light, life and legacy).

Willed action as purposeful behavior

Everything one does, all willed action, all purposeful behavior has behind it a desire to reach some end. The desire to achieve this end is the underlying motive of all willed action.

Purposeful behavior is willed action.

Only those who are free of desire, who neither aspire, nor attempt to aspire, to any greater attainment, who in short, live an uncreated life with no willed ends in view, are immune to the charm and allure of the golden Coin.

Yet even these impoverished souls must still beg. Bound to their Earthly maintenance routine by the laws of creation, they never are quite free. The concerns inherent in Earthly existence will, of necessity, create the need for willed action.

As dreamy as the eastern notion of renouncing desire to eliminate the necessity of willed action may seem, there is yet a trap involved.

To free oneself from the necessity of willed action one must free oneself from desire. In order to free oneself from desire a vast array of exercises and practices are needed, none of which lack the requirement of sustained willed effort to master.

Here the student finds that they are caught in the double bind of "desiring not to desire."

It is very difficult, at times impossible, to stop desiring something that we desire. A better method is to fulfill the desire until we no longer desire it, or until the tax outweighs the reward.

We've all had the experience of suddenly feeling like we've had enough of something. It's those moments when we watch the scales of our interest tip to the negative, and along with it our desire to do any further trading.

It's that moment at the feast when our appetite toward food turns from delight to disgust. We push the remaining scraps on the plate away saying, "Enough…karma complete."

We are all motivated by an underlying WILL, a desire for a greater state than currently exists.

It is, fundamentally, this WILL and its motivated behavior that separates Man, in capacity and value, from plants and inorganic matter.

Tending Fruit, Setting Block: Action and Production

All of Man's willed action is directed toward the attainment of ends which Man perceives as having value. The purpose of producing those ends is their capacity to result in some need or want being satisfied.

> The Pantacle of Earth, as a symbolic object, contains all the elements of earth in mixture.

Mankind's role as magician is to employ the elements in its environment as a means directed toward the achievement of its highly valued, desired ends.

To accomplish this, Man must rearrange the various elements of his environment (and perhaps his being) for the purposes of production and multiplication.

Strategy is the master's craft, transforming the Pantacle at once, into either a shield or a weapon, depending on the need of the moment.

Masters of currency circulate their means, and by this craft their means are multiplied.

Principally, the craft of strategy involves tracing the lines of cause and effect before the cause is even born.

With that knowledge, it is possible to coordinate factors of production to arrive more directly and efficiently at specific ends, typically through greater synchronicity.

This is the magical science of economics, directing elements of Earth, as means toward more valued ends, in an ever ascending evolution of value.

To accomplish this, Man's reason (Sword) informs him as to the most efficient route to take in this pursuit. In this way, Man the magician economizes his force.

The Hierarchy of Heaven: the Steps of Jacob's Ladder

As American psychologist Abraham Maslow pointed out, Man has a hierarchy of wants and needs. In order to satisfy them all in the scarce amount of time allotted to the human being requires the economizing of force. This means understanding one's scale of value and only directing one's energy/means toward attaining those ends which are of the highest value.

The Pantacle symbolizes resources. Resources are all the objects of economizing action.

The purpose of action is production. To produce anything implies a process occurring in different stages. This same is true of all ritual and initiatory developments.

For a ritual or a production process to produce results, some original factors are necessary.

From the earliest times Mankind understood that the power of its willed efforts were multiplied when it coupled together two elements: the force of its energy and labor, with the direction of some preexisting force of nature.

From this fact was born Magic, and is the driving force behind almost every religion.

For humans, this power was realized early, in simple practices such as noticing the difference in a harvest by the signs of the moon the seed was planted in. This observation of the cosmos, of its laws and patterns, is the bedrock of science, a study of causality that has led Mankind through many stages of creative endeavor from building pyramids and cathedrals, to setting loose atomic energy.

To whatever event Man intends to produce, a resource is valued because it is a direct means of satisfying an end, whether it be building an awe-inspiring monument or destroying an entire city.

This brings us to the question of how do we determine efficient and effective action, regardless of the end we desire to produce?

If Man's power is increased by aligning with those forces already existing in nature (that also support Man's same desired end) then that, from an economic standpoint, could be called a "vital market."

To plant the right seeds, at the right place, at the right time, and carefully tend them through their season, right up to the moment of harvest when those fruits will be plucked at the height of bounty by an eager hand – that is the basic recipe for spells of love and money.

The ALTAR: (WILL x WILL)

The Pantacle lies flat on the Altar, whose double cube represents the WILL of Man multiplied by the WILL of Nature. (ie. conformity with the laws of nature.)

In order for any action to produce the desired result there must be an effective *idea* of how one might use available resources as means to attain the Ritual's valued ends.

These ideas might be regarded as spells, recipes, or strategies for achievement.

Early on, when developing agriculture and the practice of smelting metals, Mankind learned that certain modes of behavior, or the observance of certain practices enabled it to attain its desired ends more predictably.

In order to progress along its evolutionary path, Mankind must have knowledge about the laws of the universe (how it operates) in order to make use of these laws to attain its desired ends with greater certainty.

This means Mankind must have certain ideas about how to achieve these ends.

These ideas may then be used to determine the behavior and effort required to effectively direct means towards ends and accomplish the desired result.

In this respect, an Individual who desires to attain a high degree of physical fitness finds that certain modes of behavior help and others hinder the fulfillment of their desired purpose.

To attain an end, and direct action toward that end, requires that an image of a desired end first be conceived.

It is this coherent image that shall be inscribed upon the Pantacle.

Without this image life is condemned to the fatal aimlessness of vegatative existence.

Without a plan all is left to circumstance.

Without willed action nothing higher can be produced.

Necessity of Life:

Man's incarnated life takes place on Earth.

Upon this Earth Mankind finds itself in a certain environment, incarnated into a certain time and bound by the force of factors invoked by those situations and circumstances called "necessity."

Surrounded by loose gravel and tossed boulders, by both fertile plains and endless deserts, by clay and mud, Man looks around at the created universe and finds that it is in disarray, only half created in respect to Man's needs and wants.

It is this situation, this environment, that Man decides to change in some way in order to fulfill the desperate ache of those needs and wants.

It is from the material elements offered by the Universe that Mankind must fulfill its most basic needs. It is from this material that the Temple must be built.

With these numerous elements found in the material environment Mankind sets to work rearranging them, in order and function, to bring about the satisfaction of desired ends.

Inevitably faced with an environment it wishes to change, Man finds there are some elements which cannot be controlled or changed, and there are those that can.

This knowledge of what is and is not possible equals knowledge of the laws of cause and effect.

The Pantacle: *A study of Cause and Effect*

All things on Earth are subject to the law of cause and effect.

The growth of Mankind into a master species means that we must gradually learn to perfect our control over the circumstances of our environment, no longer at their mercy, whether natural and social.

This requires a masterful knowledge not only of nature's laws but also of the laws inherent to human nature.

With this insight into cause and effect, consequences can be traced and inevitable implications of actions recognized before even setting the ball in motion.

In the practice of studying the cause and effect of our willed actions, we trace not only the immediate results of our actions but also the long-term results.

Willed action occurs in the present tense while being aimed at a future tense.

Like a game of billiards, there are both primary and secondary consequences to what we do. We may sink a ball or two in this turn only to set up the opponent to win the game in the next.

When we are tempted to foolishly concentrate all of our attention on some particular advantage point, while neglecting its influence on the whole of our existence, we set ourselves up for a let down of which we, ironically, would be the principal architect.

Most of Mankind's attempts at technical progress have suffered from this same theme. In trying to solve one problem ten more are created. In trying to avert a war today an even greater war is created for tomorrow. In strengthening our position on the right we open ourselves up to a flanking maneuver from the left.

Not everything that seems like an advantage is really an advantage, while some problems, if we attempt to correct them, only lead to problems of a more complex order.

Mankind invented the automobile to relieve the toil of the horse and to speed up travel. Today, fewer and fewer people keep horses, and when they do those horses can mostly be seen standing motionless in small fields with nothing in particular to do.

The desire to free a thing from its purpose leaves it with no purpose. At the same time, Mankind, choking on the fumes of its own inventions, now feels the increasing anxiety of speeding uncomfortably toward a dangerous future where the highway ends forever.

If our plans are to bear fruit which, in time, does not become rotten and brown, we must bear in mind the law of cause and effect and the primary and secondary consequences of our actions.

In this Earthly sphere of time and space, economic action is that which is driven by logistics. This means that we look into the crystal ball of cause and effect and execute our plans based on IF…THEN statements.

This is the role of strategy. It is the Art of forming the Pantacle.

Ends and Means: Program Planning

When a person feels aimless it's often because they have no well-defined plan. Unconscious of their True WILL, they don't even know where to start.

In this regard, True WILL represents one's conscious order. Thus, it becomes the model for all planning.

Since this section deals with the Pantacle, the following paragraphs will continue likewise in cause and effect fashion, advancing "as-if" the reader is already conscious of where their energy is directed. That's to say, they already possess an inherent knowledge of their main aim in life, their True WILL.

This means that they possess the clarity to formulate this aim clearly and precisely. This aim will naturally include some goal to be reached.

To reach this goal it will be necessary for the Individual to remain "true" to its end, and adapt as needed to the goal's changing trajectory, continuing through all the long (and sometimes complex) stages and processes involved in its execution and ultimate fulfillment without swerving or getting pulled off course by the myriad of: blind ways, bluffs, obstacles, raging rivers, endless deserts, dark forests and false summits that one may encounter on their incarnated trip through space and time.

This can happen at many stages in the development of a project or idea.

One finds that certain things are required to complete the project, and so they go off to obtain those things only to find that obtaining those things indirectly requires other things not originally considered necessary, and to obtain those things requires actions and resources that require still others, and on and on in a seemingly endless chain of necessity until one can barely remember what they first started out to do.

> The danger is that means tend to become ends in themselves.

Central to this problem is money. Money is the primary means to an end, and for that reason tends to become an end in itself. Here the tendency is to amass money without having any idea of how to employ it usefully.

Many a Man has become enslaved by the means he has chosen to employ to attain his ends.

War may be used as a means to preserve a nation, or when it becomes an end in itself, to utterly destroy that nation.

This trend of Man being enslaved by the means he uses, is quite evident in technology where intelligent machines are created to increase man's powers yet now lord over the species as a sort of independent, superior and uncontrollable threat.

The antidote for this is for Mankind to develop a vigilant and energetic WILL, one capable of keeping means in their place.

This means using means, while also remaining master of them, using only those means that truly serve our intended purpose, and only to the extent that they continue to serve it.

In regard to hierarchy, the Pantacle is directed by and subordinate to the WILL.

There is a hierarchy of needs.

First and most basic are personal and psychological needs (Pantacle) and then transpersonal or meta-needs (Cup).

Fulfilling the first, paradoxically, often leads to a state of boredom, emptiness, and meaninglessness. This is the existential vacuum, an inner void.

A focus on meta-needs tends to lead to peak-experiences (Nietzsche's Ubermensch), while a focus on lower needs tends to descend to an abyss-experience (Nietzsche's Last Man).

The meta-needs represent the need for understanding the meaning of life.

The opposite is the hum-drum of constant earthly dissatisfaction and sense of futility that arises when a person finds themselves constantly coming up against the pointed hedge of mundane limitations.

In its seemingly aimless cycles the cosmic rubble-clod called Earth achingly turns its rusty grinding wheel, squeaking and moaning on its axis as the friction of orbit comes up against the rough edges of a material existence without direction or meaning.

In such a state, having time tends to feel like "doing time." This is the prison of a life that has no higher purpose, a donkey ride over a monotonous rough, rocky plain with no peak-experiences in sight.

It is both the drama and glory of Man that this higher level of consciousness, sooner or later, demands satisfaction. Every need arouses, sooner or later, a corresponding WILL.

The Dice:

"Alea iacta est." (The die is cast)
- attributed to Julius Caesar as he crossed the Rubicon

This world is a world of uncertainty. We shall never be able to forecast the future course of the world with precision. Time and time again, the future course of history has been decided by a roll of the dice. Unpredictability can be a powerful influence. The runes Hagalaz and Perthro are the names of these dice.

Man never has certain knowledge of the future. There is an unsetting reality here. Despite our scientific research, high-tech algorithms, and generational sense of superiority to the past, life and the future of consciousness must ever make its peace with the uncertainty that is at the root of material creation.

It is an uncertainty born of the unpredictability inherent in human nature, our insufficient knowledge of the unconscious nature of ourselves, our insufficient knowledge of natural phenomena, including the inner workings of the cosmos, as well as our inability to comprehend what Carl Jung called "the Spirit of the Depths" which secretly guides the hand of fate and the necessities of both personal and collective karma.

As a result, all of our prudent, carefully calculated actions are, nonetheless, speculations. The future is uncertain. Thus, human existence is framed within the context of a fundamental implication: Mystery.

This means that, in regard to human action, the omnipresence of uncertainty includes the ever-present possibility of the unknown.

Every action, therefore, involves risk. This risk cannot be eliminated.

Life is a sand castle licked by the tides of a great ocean.

Many attempts at fulfilling one's calling may need to be made and much undeserved abuse may be received along the way, yet the Pantacle of Life keeps spinning toward new dawns and new days in a relentless renewal of second chances.

Turning with it, round and round, is the Wheel of Fortune; patterns and rhythms of luck and opportunity that keep rising and falling: like the breath in one's lungs, like tides of the ocean, like empires of the East.

Contained in the Pantacle is the crust of centuries.

Concealed in the gravel of parking lots are the ground up bones of dinosaurs, dragons, and giants sacrificed in the ancient but ever renewing body of Earth's mythic creation.

The world's history is long, and along the way the tail-eating serpent of time has digested much of the content of its beginnings. Along the way there have been entire continents sunk or torn apart in terrestrial acts of conclusive destruction, and along with them the forgotten remembrance of endless ages and vistas of Man.

Although the scrolls written of those great times no longer exist, carefully preserved copies remain forever lodged in the labyrinth-like libraries of the Individual's own unconscious mind. The substance of the material world hangs on a mythic frame.

The understructure of reality is a psychedelic rabbit hole, virtually without end.

This vault is vast. No matter how deep our investigation into the Pantacle cuts we could only ever scratch the surface.

Despite the jewel-filled caverns and treasures of Earth, material reality is also the root of incarnated suffering. This was the realization of Siddhartha when he first left the royal palace. Experiences of wealth and poverty, abundance and hunger, youth and old age, birth and death are inevitable experiences during the course of natural life.

In both Gnosticism and Buddhism, Earth is viewed as a sort of prison where the incarnated are held in bondage to physical existence, with the chains of this bondaged forged of those Individual links of needs, wants, and desires.

In the Tarot this concept is symbolized by *the Devil* card, associated with Capricorn, that time of year when the arc of the Sun descends low on the horizon and matter temporarily seems to reign over spirit.

These religious ideas reflect a sort of enlightened pessimism about the ultimate nature of material existence. What both these perspectives intuit are the limitations of matter, expressed in the limitations imposed by matter on consciousness.

What almost every spiritual tradition emphasizes is that matter, in all its reality, in fact holds no reality outside its intercourse with consciousness.

What exists for consciousness is only that which makes itself known to consciousness. Philosopher Arthur Schopenhaur also emphasized this point in his book titled *The World as Will and Representation*.

"The World is my Idea, this is a truth which holds good for everything that lives and knows, though Man alone can bring it into reflective and abstract consciousness. If he really does this, he has attained to philosophical wisdom.

It then becomes clear and certain to him that what he knows is not a Sun and an Earth but only an eye that sees a Sun, a hand that feels an Earth."

The Pantacle is about the *embodiment* of Spirit in the manifest world of forms. It's about the incarnation of ideas, and through them, the ongoing aggrandizement of consciousness itself.

We can only add to the World by adding to consciousness, everything else is just the reshaping of recycled material.

From this material, blocks are hewn in service of the Great Work. From this material of Earth a pyramid ascends in service of consciousness, guided by the eye and hand of a higher intelligence.

The Eye that sees the Sun perceives its Daimon, shining down, with helping hands on rays of life. The hand that feels the Earth, perceives a part of itself in the material being sculpted, and like its own history, gives old material a new shape.

Like the mythic ouroboros serpent with its tail in its mouth, life, it seems, is but an endless chase, an endless task – both the work and its reward, both the hunt and the feast.

On the Royal Road, both the journey and its destination at last become one.

One is the Spirit, of Self, Daimon, and Sun

One is their WILL, conjoined in ends

One is the Cup: sacrificing life so life might drink

One is the Mind, dividing creation for a chance at love's union

One is the body of Man, uniting two hands in a single operation,

---

…tending to the completion of the Great Work…
forever and ever… until the end of time.

Tools of the Royal Art:

Traditionally the Pantacle is a flat disk of beeswax, symbolizing the toil (like the bees) of material existence. Implied also is the nectar of existence, the honey from which the sacred mead of the Gods is brewed.

Ritual Practices:

The Principal Rituals of the Pantacle are rituals of physical and material development. These include any and all acts of building and all acts where an economy of action is necessary. To these ends, all styles and degrees of physical exercise and physical fitness go here.

The Pantacle and the Ritual of Strength and Health:

Weights are ritual tools whose purpose lives in their ability to effectively invoke the god of strength, "Magna Vitalitas."

Typically, the physical moments in this type of ritual involve repeated motions, with very specific emphasis on the weight of the ritual tool (rather than its beauty) as a demonstration of each initiate's own ever-escalating struggle with "The Dragon" of its epic mythology.

The physical ritual is structured so that the Initiate aids his God in a mythic battle to triumph against this terrible, herculean beast whose latin name is, "Magna Gravitas."

By way of a continued ritualized engagement, weapons in the form of magic hammers, bars, plates, barbells, ropes, weighted balls, and various other iron-made accessories, are wielded against this dragon, in a drama of sweat and exertion framed within the context of the broader metaphoric struggle fundamental to life itself.

Framing the ritual in this context forms the spiritualization mythos of physicality's religion. One of its chief saints, to whom many devotees pray, is St. Discipline.

Struggle after struggle, ritual after ritual, with each ritual a struggle and each struggle a ritual, the initiate of physical rites strives to become both Warrior and Magician, invoking the powers of food and supplement, macro and micro nutrients, in a ritual of incremental increase for the definite purpose of invoking the spirit and power of its god into physical form.

To this end, positive exertion is the central sacrifice, with the capstone of every act being a devotion to the perfect form and health of Magna Vitalitas, the supreme god of Earth.

The Priests of this Temple have knowledge of spells, acceptable sacrifices, and how specific rituals can be performed to best please Magna Vitalitas.

Most sacrifices are burnt upon the altar in one's own Temple, the body.

The ancient mythic structure, embodied in physicality's initiation rituals suggests that the blessings of Magna Vitalitas must be won by each initiate through acts of devotion to the god.

The sacred incense of this cult is produced by the combustion of "caloric units" sacrificed during the vigorous performance of the ritual itself.

From this comes its sacred fragrance, born of devotional sweating.

Rituals and sacrifices of this element are highly enhanced through repetition, occurring frequently, even daily. Once again, in this cult, a very specific emphasis is put on the measurement of weights, values consumed, and the rituals' duration of time.

Some rituals to the God of Strength may be performed on altars in the shape of benches, that can be either flat or inclined.

Sometimes it is the precise tally of movements, also called "reps," that its members conclude are the good omens of a positive outcome for their sacrifice.

The god of Health and Strength frequently receives offerings in the form of food of some symbolic type, most pleasing when it has been specialty portioned.

Some sacrifices are said to have been blessed with a positive spirit, or "vitamin" which the God of Strength covets.

Many of these sacrificial offerings are chosen for how well they burn when added to the basin in the sacrificial altar at the center of their sacred temple, which they call "the Body."

Other Rituals of the Pantacle include those with obvious connections with economics.

The Ritual of Economics

This ritual operates as a system or place of business where goods, services or knowledge are exchanged for profit. The daily operations of the business are its rituals. Its ledgers and account books are the ritualized recordings of the ritual proceedings.

Brands are talismans, logos are symbolic spirits whose purpose is to influence perception and emotion in the human mind. Advertising and Marketing are the craft of invoking the spirit of psychology and constraining its power to live within persuasive spells or influential talismans, also called "ads."

Correspondence, emails, advertising and verbal communications are composed of letters and words, spells whose purpose is to communicate with spirits (clients, customers, colleagues) for the purposes of exchanging knowledge, information and material goods.

Suppliers, clients and customers are transactionary spirits whose relation is confined to their particular element(s) and based primarily on matters of value exchange. Storefronts are temples to the familial spirit of the business.

Offices are ritual workspaces for writing spells and making transactions with spirits. Many of these transactions are now with spirits capable of communicating from great distances, their speech instantaneously arriving through the air by way of call, text or email.

The God of the Economic Ritual is – $ a symbol that represents the serpent coiled in supremacy around the Tree-of-Life.

Practical Matters

The Pantacle defines the practical concerns of everyday life. This... Is... Reality.

The "Practicality" factor of every other weapon is its direct relation to the physical world. If a thing can't be made to touch life and leave its fingerprint, then it's not real enough to matter much.

If a weapon's force can not be brought to bear on reality, on substance, and on the nitty-gritty points of life, then its force and power will remain essentially conceptual, and be barred from the gates of the actual.

In the end, everything has to make sense on a practical level if it is ever to come into being for any real duration of time. If something is to endure, then it must conform with the trueness of an enduring Universal Law.

Ill-conceived, unbalanced, highly deformed urges do occasionally break though the collective veil and transform the inert masses into a mental force with its own temporary momentum.

Advancing from a thought to a frenzy, with only a short slogan and some simple colored stripes to give it form and hold its disparate elements together, these movements are almost entirely volatile and destructive. Yet these convulsions are the masses' only experience of power in the material world.

Adolescent impulses of this type quickly bring with them a lot of lessons.

These lessons become the small knicks, scratches, bumps and scars that the wax pantacle receives in its encounters with the world.

The Pantacle's lesson here is that the mental sphere of ideas and the imaginative sphere of creative inspirations, are not the same as the material world, and they don't follow the same rules or laws of operation.

Creative matters are creative matters. Emotional matters are emotional matters. Financial matters are financial matters.

When financial matters become emotional matters then emotional matters become financial matters and a cycle starts spinning.

Earthly life is made up of a lot of different elements, emotions, thoughts, experiences, and trash. In reality the Earth is a lightly molded piece of cosmic rubble.

There are some things that don't mix well. They have reactionary natures and are better kept apart from each other. Lit matches and open gasoline cans are one such example. Finances and emotions are another.

Making important decisions from a levelheaded, grounded, practically minded perspective is what was once termed the "virtue of prudence."

When we want to create something that functions well in the World, then that thing, idea, dream, inspiration, hope, longing, drive, desire, or WILL must be brought forth into reality in accord and alignment with the established guidelines of natural law. That is, if it's meant to last.

Building projects can move forward quickly if what's being built is meant to collapse.

Things can be brought into being quickly, no doubt. It's really a question of staying power. Who can bring into creation that which will endure for more than just a short span of time?

Endurance is not postmodern culture's strong point. Fads are its strong point.

The word "Fad" finds its eytomological origins in the latin 'fatuus' which means stupid. Like the sugar rush that feeds it, it begins with great energy and ends in a catastrophic flop.

Contemporary culture is both recycled and disposable. It has no staying power and was never meant to last. That's a big problem.

Never in the history of civilization has there been so much infrastructure that was never built to last. When building roads for life's journey, it seems "the long haul" has failed to be considered.

If we were to look into humanity's collective inventory of assets right now, we would see a whole lot of packaged produce, turning quickly, with visible spots of mold.

In this sense, humanity's harvest basket is full AND going bad.

The Pantacle is about long-term thinking, about seeing the bigger picture in things and understanding how systems affect each other.

How do those kinds of clouds mean there will be rain in three days?

How do we fix big problems?

How do we fix the world?

How do we fix the fence on the other side of the farm when there's still wood to chop and pigs to feed?

Practical Matters have followed Man since the species' birth.

The Royal Art is about mixing enough magic with enough dirt to give an idea life.

It's about taking a creative lightning flash from up above and incarnating it in form.

That represents 99% of the task on the Great Work's to–do list.

CHAPTER SIX

God's Plan, THE HEXAGRAM

The Order of Heaven

The hexagon is an aesthetic and geometric symbol, typically conceived with an equilateral, symmetrical form, coming near to a circle while still possessing angles and forming a nexus at which matter and consciousness converge and intersect. This is the union of fire and water, matter and spirit, God and Man.

The Hexagon thus represents a unity of opposites. It is the symbolic uniting of two opposing forces or concepts. In its aesthetic harmony it symbolizes the unity of dual forces, the ability for one to complement the other and synthesize and integrate their opposing natures into one coherent entity.

> All symbols are a connecting point between matter and consciousness.

They are energetic arrangements that correspond with some idea, concept, or meaning.

By the fact that all perceived matter is interpreted by consciousness, all matter can potentially be seen as symbolic. In this sense, the hexagon might be thought of as a symbol of symbolism, a symbol of the Universe's inherent symbolic order.

A symbol is something that has meaning and the hexagon's inherent aesthetic symbolism is deeply tied with the question of meaning. The meaning of meaning is that something stands in for something else.

The question of what's the meaning of life is answered by the symbolic definition of meaning: one thing means another, one thing stands in for another, one thing becomes another, and in this way the meaning of the hexagram is that everything is connected. When Man the Pentagram is united with the Hexagram, *the Will of Man and God become ONE.*

It is the conjunction of the pentagram with the hexagram that gives life a transcendent meaning. It is the place where Individual meaning and universal meaning converge. In other words, the synchronization of Heaven and Earth.

Attaining and maintaining this state of unified consciousness (which bestows powers to influence nature) was essential to the original, Sovereign Spiritual System.

As the mediator between the two realms, Pharaoh wore the double Crown.

As in the time of Pharaoh, the Sovereign was the mediator between Heaven and Earth. The Sovereign held back the tides of flood and chaos, bringing rain and plenty, uniting with the land (in the form of the Queen), and begetting the bounty of blessings that sustained the Kingdom.

With the Sovereign's consciousness in rapport with the greater processes of life, the Sovereign's actions take on a transcendent meaning. These meaningful, ritualized actions then produce effects.

The state of the Kingdom was understood to be a mirror reflection of the state of the Sovereign. A Kingdom is a reflection of the "state of consciousness" that rules it.

"When the righteous are in authority, the people rejoice: but when the wicked beareth rule, the people mourn."
- Proverbs 29:2

If the Kingdom loses its sense of transcendent meaning, it means the Sovereign has failed in their sacred duties.

If the Sovereign fails to impart meaning and order upon the Kingdom, it will succumb to chaos, fall to foreign influence and become a submissive client state to outside interest. The fruit of the Kingdom will be harvested by foreign hands, its treasures will be picked apart as spoils of conquest, and its memories dispersed by the sands of time. In short, the Kingdom will fall to ruins.

Where life has lost its sense of greater meaning, where God does not exist, where the connection and harmony between things has not yet been established, there the hexagon symbolizes the necessity to create this connection.

"Where there is no vision the people perish:
but he that keepeth the law, happy is he."
- Proverbs 29:18

In this regard the hexagon represents the stable, connecting center of the Universe, the coherence (or Law) that ties and links everything together. Coordinated with the Pentagram, *the Will of Man connects with the Will of the All.*

Understood through the coherent unity of the hexagon, everything is given meaning by the interconnectedness of the conscious universe. It symbolizes a universe in which things are already elementally perfect, yet Man is charged with perfecting the arrangement of those elements.

Closely tied to this idea is the Jungian concept of synchronicity, a psychological term that points to a benevolent singularity already existing in the universe and capable of guiding us in orchestrated movements with timed precision. Inherent in this idea is the need to consciously align ourselves with this universal synchronicity. In this we find much of the meaning of Magick.

The hexagon is a compromise between a polygon and a circle, and for this reason honeybees use its shape to cover and create open areas while minimizing boundaries, thus it minimizes the amount of material needed to build these boundaries. Divinity expresses itself in efficiency.

Every polygon has an equilateral form, with the angles equally divided and congruent, but not the hexagon. Add any more sides to a hexagon and it's more circular than polygonal. Subtract any more sides and it's more polygonal than circular.

As the universal average, the hexagon creates the best possible torque for mechanical engineering. It is the exact middle compromise between a three-sided polygon, and an infinite-sided shape like a circle.

This makes hexagons structurally stable. The regularity and evenness of their shape allows hexagons to repeat, while their near-circularity allows maximum perfect load distribution.

The hexagon is the exact compromise between the equality of a circle (perfect symmetry on all sides with all points an equal distance from the center) and the angles of a polygon. Functionally this is best for the distribution of load and stress, thus it becomes the axle upon which the manifest universe turns.

A Symbol of Time

The hexagon can also be said to represent time.

The symbol's compromise between polygonality and circularity reflects the nature and rhythm of time. As the wheel of the year, it represents the alternations of time through seasonal shifts.

Space and time are closely related, with time being needed to bring about events. The hexagon's perfect compromise between polygonality and circularity implies something about the nature of time itself; it occasionally contains a rhythm of its own interruption.

In terms of physics, time is distance. In this regard, the end of time (Apocalypse/Ragnarok) means everything collapses into one point. At this point, all of creation becomes united in the life-giving, death throes of an ecstatic battle.

The climax of this event is what the French call *petite mort*, or in English – the orgasm.

God *(An omni-effective force)* **beyond Reason**

Like an orgasm, this "little death" is the experience of the Godhead, crown or unity that transcends the bounds of Reason.

This says something about the nature of the God-concept, which is ultimately a trans-conceptual force promulgated through the mystery of light.

It is because of this "mystery" and the inherent trans-conceptual nature of the God concept that its "Reason" must forever remain hidden from our vision. We have a very difficult time conceptually capturing it because it operates according to "laws" that transcend reason.

It operates outside of Reason. Its central governing law is a loophole of law, thus it is Sovereign. In this sense it represents that which is above law because *it is the source of law.*

The Daimon, here conceptualized as a Sun image with hands on rays of light, represents the being or state superior in relation to where the Individual is currently.

It is an omni-effectual force operating both through Reason's laws *and* the hidden laws of synchronicity. Like the Solar Cross, it is the conjunction of a horizontal and vertical axis, the meeting of predictability with chance, a unison of known factors with unknown possibilities.

This points to the existence of a necessary *Being*, state, or current of communication capable of bridging the gap between Earth and Heaven, between the mundane and the transcendent spheres of existence.

It is this Being that carries a message from the higher sphere to the lower and delivers it as the Individual's "Call" or motive of WILL. This prompts the Individual toward some willed action that they may only partially understand.

Subjectively, the WILL is felt as the raw expression of a divine and mysterious force, seeking fulfillment. The Holy Cup, the supreme object of its fulfillment, gives the WILL its direction.

This is what puts the 'holy' in the Holy Grail. It is the manifesting cauldron, giving conceptual shape to a trans-conceptual force. It takes the Spirit of God, and conceives a form for its manifestation, an image.

When this image receives its "coat of skin," the Spirit of God becomes incarnated as Man, a Sun of God.

Following the ordained pattern of the Golden Ratio, this is the birth of God's spirit in the body of Man.

The Crown: Unity of consciousness

A supreme Godhead is an absolute necessity of existence that cannot be negated or divided by Reason because it is the unifying reality upon which the whole structure of Reason rests and operates.

The only true way of comprehending the nature of this mysterious force (respective to the Individual) is through one's True WILL, which might be thought of as the subjective validity of a transcendent, objective reality.

It is by virtue that one has a WILL, which longs for the object of its aspiration, that life exists. This is the connection between WILL and LOVE.

Without this mysterious force there would be no drive for experience. The tree would not branch, the bird would not nest, the bee would not buzz.

Life originates in the flames of the Sun. Its WILL is reflected in the Sun in Man.

The unity of the pentagram and hexagram, the microcosm and macrocosm, overcomes the dualistic conceptions that divide both life and consciousness. The Sword of Reason has, throughout history, been the principal agent of this division.

The Sword represents division and hence a knowledge and separation of life into good and evil, left and right, divine and mundane. In the hexagram we go, in Neitzche's words, beyond good and evil, with the two becoming one.

Taken far enough, Reason returns to and then necessarily loses itself to mystery.

Mystery is that which is beyond duality and the faculties of Reason. The chronically reasonable person fears this is insanity. In truth, this state represents a mystical reality, the true foundation of all reality.

Attaining the awareness of a trans-conceptual function, or in other words a "vision of the Grail," affirms the mystery which is the nourishment of existence. The substance of this mystery is light.

Here we return again to the Sun. To grasp the power of this God-force, it's necessary to accept its conceptual frame as being out of, and beyond, this World. It represents the symbolic principle for the highest possible unity of experience in consciousness.

Like the Sun, this highest cause is of a magnitude that is beyond earthly comparison or estimation. It is of a sphere above all that is possible to reason, and so, is also free from the self-contradiction of reason. That is both its power and the substance of its perfection.

For the Solar Individual, aligning with this highest cause via their True WILL is to be raised to a sphere beyond the limits and contradictions of reason. It lives in a realm where arguments cannot touch it.

A person's WILL emits from a mysterious place, and yet it is synchronistically in tune with a hidden order. This is Sovereignty… the unified crown of creation.

The Highest Cause

Because no one has "all experience," the absolute properties of one's destiny cannot be deduced or reasoned from experience alone.

Therefore, the explanations of reason are insufficient to tie down these sublime forces. WILL, like life, is fed by a mysterious river of unknown origins.

For the Sovereign Individual, True WILL is the expression of the *highest cause* of their existence. This both deifies the Individual's nature and becomes the source which constantly renews their strength.

The Sun represents the unity of nature. It is the creative expression of the Godhead which bridges the gap between Nature and that which lies beyond Nature – its cause.

This cause, the "highest cause," is the principle which introduced, via light, the aims and ends of consciousness into the physical World.

The hands of the divine Author descend as rays of the Sun.

Dipping its quill into the cosmic inkwell, the divine Author (like Sir Francis Bacon writing the plays of Shakespeare) produces tremendously complex works with a mysterious hand, often under assumed names. These assumed names are those heroes, kings and prophets "whose names perish not."

Authoring both tragedies and comedies, ending in both death and marriage, the creative spirit resurrects itself again and again, in new stories, new sagas, new books, and occasionally – even a New God Image.

Science or Sovereignty

The creation of the World, from a scientific perspective, is the product of chance – a series of fortunate coincidences. Yet at its heart this perspective also implies a sort of mysterious, uncanny synchronicity.

The odds of a complex creation coming into being without a creator are so out of proportion to reason's jurisdiction as to hint at a mathematical proof that existence has an underlying, though mysterious, Author.

In other words, *the creation of the Universe requires the existence of a God-force*, both operating outside the limits of reason and unbound in its creative capacity by the laws of mere physical causality.

If this God-force was completely subject to rational, mechanical laws then it would be limited by the terms of its own creation. The laws of creation would then be as handcuffs to the creativity of the creator.

> No wise being would willingly create inescapable limits for itself.

Chance and synchronicity are cooperational. What we call chance is a loophole through which an independent force can operate. Chance is an open door for the free-will of the God-force to step through. This is the power of the "dice"– an opportunity to gain freedom from the constraints of pure reason.

Sovereignty: freedom from the constraints of pure reason

Even after we have attained the highest summit of knowledge, we find language insufficient to adequately express the conception of the whole.

Reason, investigating causes and effects constantly (and necessarily) bases its analysis on comparisons to "some other thing" in an infinite chain of comparison that eventually gives way to an abyss of nothingness (existential crisis) unless we admit there is a higher form of Sovereignty.

This Sovereignty is expressed in *a supreme meaning or Being* that is both primal and self-subsistent. In short, the recognition of a force that does not depend on, nor is limited by, the reasons of this World.

The call of True WILL represents the Individual's article of faith, and yet as always, this faith transcends reason. Depending on reason for faith requires a person to seek an ungraspable explanation, some solid factual ground for everything that exists, or else their faith collapses into an atheistic nihilism.

Atheism is the ultimate product of unrestrained reason. It was science's mishandling of the Sword of Reason that originally "killed God." Since then that same Sword has served to severely maim society as a whole.

Attacking the God-concept, the Sword as a weapon of division, attempts to divide that which by essence and definition is a unity. The Mind ponders the stars of the night sky and is bewildered, none of its calculations can compare with infinity.

The Mind's attempts to comprehend the incomprehensible only leads to a breakup of the assumed supremacy of Reason, in other words insanity.

Faced with this unsettling fact, and unable to conjoin the pentagram with the hexagram in any reasonable way, the modern mind finds itself recoiling in existential horror.

Here, it became much easier to suggest that a God-force "does not exist," than for Reason to be forced into a showdown with the infinite, leading to a traumatic and humiliating defeat.

In hierarchical fashion, Reason must bend its knee to the incomprehensible. Reason must acknowledge that some things cannot be fully understood, much less explained. Reason is able to dominate many situations, but its powers of understanding are indeed limited.

Reason bridges the abyss that separates causes and conditions of the lower order (science) from the higher order which precedes it in origin (the mystical God-force).

To get why this is important, it's necessary to grasp that the transcendental idea is so immeasurably great, so high above all, that it stands apart from the series of natural causes, or reasons confined to mere material causality. This is the mysterious force that guides the axle of universal synchronicity.

The Sun, or Solar force, is the conductor of the orchestra of the Solar System. It is the force of synchronicity that weaves together the threads of unexplainable occurrences that first created life, and continues to do so.

The Individual, thus aligned with this cosmic symphony through the current of their True WILL is no longer depressed by doubts of impoverished reason. They have succeeded in liberating themselves from the existential prison of debilitating uncertainty.

The Sun is the symbol of certainty.

Unshackled from the deep doubt of reasoned nihilism, the Individual rises like the Sun.

All great goals begin as "unreasonable," because they stretch the boundaries of what is possible. This is the domain of inspiration, courage, genius, and adventure.

EPILOGUE

CLOSING THE CIRCLE

> "The Self always has the quality of eternity, and a circle is the symbol of eternity."
> - Carl Jung, The synthesis of the four elements

"The Circle is at times synonymous with circumference, just as the circumference is often equated with circular movement. But although its general meaning embraces both aspects, there are some further details which it's important to emphasize. The circle or disk is, very frequently, an emblem of the Sun (and indisputably so when it is surrounded by rays). It also bears a certain relationship to the number ten (symbolizing the return to unity from multiplicity) when it comes to stand for heaven and perfection and sometimes eternity as well.

Enclosing beings, objects or figures within a circumference has a double meaning: from within, it implies limitation and definition; from without, it is seen to represent the defense of physical and psychic contents themselves against the perils of the soul threatening it from without, these dangers being, in a way, tantamount to chaos, but more particularly to illimitation and disintegration. Circumferential movement, which the Gnostics turned into one of their basic emblems

> *by means of the figure of the dragon, or serpent biting its tail, is a representation of time. The Ouroboros (the circle formed by a dragon biting its own tail) is to be found in the Codex Marcianus which explains how its meaning embraces all cyclic systems. The alchemist took up this Gnostic symbol and applied it to the process of their symbolic* **opus** *of human destiny."*
>
> - A Dictionary of Symbols, J.E. Cirlot

"The CIRCLE announces the Nature of the Great Work."

He (the Magician) chooses a Circle rather than any other lineal figure for many reasons:

1. He affirms thereby his identity with the infinite.
2. He affirms the equal balance of his working, since all points on the circumference are equidistant from the centre.
3. He affirms the limitation implied by his devotion to the Great Work. He no longer wanders about aimlessly in the World.

- Aleister Crowley, Book 4

The Temple: *the circumference of Man*

Manly P. Hall, excerpts from *The Secret Teachings of all Ages*:

The Mysteries of every nation taught that the laws, elements, and powers of the Universe were epitomized in the human constitution; that everything which existed outside of Man had its analogue within Man.

As the natural outgrowth of this practice there was fabricated a secret theological system in which God was considered as the Grand Man and, conversely, Man as the little God.

Early priests caused the statue of a Man to be placed in the sanctuary of the Temple. This human figure symbolized the Divine Power in all its intricate manifestations. Thus the priests of antiquity accepted Man as their textbook, and through the study of him learned to understand the greater and more abstruse mysteries of the celestial scheme of which they were a part.

As Man's physical body has five distinct and important extremities – two legs, two arms, and a head, of which the last governs the first four – the number 5 has been accepted as the symbol of man. By its four corners the Pyramid symbolizes the arms and legs, and by its apex the head, thus indicating that one rational power controls four irrational corners. The hands and feet are used to represent the four elements, of which the two feet are earth and water, and the two hands fire and air. The brain then symbolizes the sacred fifth element – æther – which controls and unites the other four. If the feet are placed together and the arms outspread, Man then symbolizes the cross with the rational intellect as the head or upper limb.

The philosophers of antiquity realized that Man himself was the key to the riddle of life, for he was the living image of the Divine Plan, and in future ages humanity also will come to realize more fully the solemn import of those ancient words: *The proper study of Mankind is Man.*

The body of Man must not be considered as the Individual but only as the house of the Individual, in the same manner that the Temple was the House of God.

CIRCUMAMBULATION

So then Man, holding the Golden Ratio within your hands, who draws *you*?

With your arms and legs stretched and sketched upon an Earthly vellum, sprawled upon a circle, following lines and angles in conformity to divine proportions, what then is the truth upon which your nature is conceived?

If the Pentagram is the sign of your true spirit, Man, then what are you?

Devil or God?

Or something balanced perfectly in between?!

Answer the question Man, now once and for all!

Do you see the sign and hear "The Call?"

Is the Golden Ratio true? Are you in accord with its Law as the living embodiment of ALL?

The Sphinx's great riddle is you, the eternal spirit of the Anthropocosmos…the god within God called *Universal Man.*

THIS BOOK AS A PANTACLE

This book is composed like a pentagram: as a set of lines drawn from point to point, intersecting at precise angles.

There are points where they start and points where they end, and points where they cross each other giving form to its shape and design.

These points are the enlightened perspectives of many authors and great thinkers across the ages.

As the author of this book, my task has been simply to connect these points, like an archeologist might reassemble the blocks of an ancient Temple.

Likewise, the work here has been dedicated to the resurrecting of that Temple's lost mythic image – *The Sun in Man*.

This image remains an ever-present reality, deeply rooted in consciousness, behind and beyond the world that changes.

As a divine inheritance, the Golden Ratio is alive in Man.

The human body is the intersection of four elements, crowned with Spirit and superimposed upon the Universal Plan.

Guided by the light of one's *Sun Within*, the Rod, the Cup, the Sword, and the Pantacle represent the 'elemental parts' of oneself, in their purest expression.

The Rod is the force of pure Fire, the hollow tube through which the creative fire passes – the channel of its current. It represents the pure drive, the most powerful impulse to do one's "True Will."

The Cup represents the force of pure Water, the baptism of initiation, a vessel of gnosis, the bestower of grace. It represents the primal womb, the purifying effects of water, and the pure reception and reflection of one's Highest Understanding.

The Sword represents the force of pure Air, the gleaming razor-sharp, double-edged blade of Reason, holding enemies on point. It represents the force of the human mind when balanced and controlled, whose every stroke is as clearly and singularly cut as its grasp is firmly motivated by Love and WILL.

The Pantacle represents the force of Pure Earth, the fertile ground of manifestation: our Senses, the medium of the artist, the substance upon which one makes an impression. It represents the material world, the body, time, and the inherent chain of cause and effect from which life is built. It is both the toiling labor in the fields of earthly life and the buttered bread of its harvest.

Like the writing of this book, the ritual of Man involves tracing the lines of the pentagram from one point to the next so that the power of opposing elements can all be brought to bear on one object of service and united with the plan of the ALL.

The object of that service is the ascending consciousness of Man the Pentagram; whose power ignites fire, stills water, commands air, and hews blocks of stone from the Earth. These blocks rise, one by one, building the Temple that shall be the holy house for that indomitable spirit: *The Sun in Man*.

Etymological foundations of chapter concepts:

CHAPTER ONE: THE DAIMON

SOL - the Sun personified (Daimon), Proto-Indo-European "whole, well-kept, Solace, comfort."

AUTHOR (n.)
Someone who originates or causes or initiates something, be the author of, to do or originate. Mid-14c, *auctor, autour, autor* "father, creator, one who brings about, one who makes or creates" Latin *auctor* "promoter, producer, progenitor; builder, founder," literally "one who causes growth" from Proto-Indo-European root **aug* "to increase."

AUTHENTIC (adj.)
Authenticated, not counterfeit, mid-14c., *autentik,* "authoritative, duly, authorized," Old French *autentique* "authentic, canonical," Latin *authenticus*, from Greek *authentikos* "original, genuine, principal," from *authentes* "one acting on one's own authority," form *autos* "self" +*hentes* "does, being."

AUTHORITY (n.)
Freedom from doubt; belief in yourself and your abilities, official permission or approval, an authoritative written work. Old French *autorité, auctorité,* "authority, prestige, right, permission, dignity, gravity," Latin *auctoritatem* "influence, command," from *auctor* "master, leader, author." From c. 1300 in the general sense of "legal validity," also "authoritative book; authoritative doctrine," from mid-14c. As "right to rule or command, power or right to command or act." In Middle English aslo, "power derived from good reputation, official sanction."

AUTARCHY (n.)
1600s, "absolute sovereignty," from Latinized form of Greek *autarkhia*, form *autarkhein* "to be an absolute ruler," from *autos* "self + *arkein* "to rule."

ARCHON (n.)
From Greek arkhon "ruler, commander, chief, captain, arkein "be the first," thence "to begin, begin from or with, make preparation for," also "to rule, lead the way, govern." One of the nine chief magistrates of ancient Athens.

DICTATE (v.)
Issue commands or orders for, say out loud for the purpose of recording, past participle of dictare "say often, prescribe, to say, speak," from Proto-Indo-European root *deik - "to show, to pronounce solemnly." 1590s, "positive order or command," 1610s "authoritative rule, maxim, or precept."

GENIUS (n.)
Late 14c., "tutelary or moral spirit" who guides and governs an individual through life, from Latin *genius* "guardian deity or spirit which watches over each person from birth, spirit, incarnation, wit, talent," also "prophetic skill; the male spirit of *gens,*" originally "generative power" (or "inborn nature") from Proto-European *gen(e)-yo-, from root gene - "give, birth, beget." from 1580's sense of "characteristic disposition."

CHARACTER (n.)
Mid-14c., character, "symbol marked or branded on the body," mid-15c., "symbol or drawing in sorcery," late 15c.

CALL (v.)
Mid-13c., "to cry out; call for, summon, invoke, ask for, demand, order, give a name to, apply by way of designation," from Old Norse kalla "to cry loudly, summon in a loud voice, name, call by name."

DEITY (n.)
C. 1300, *deite*, "divine nature, godhood, attributes of a god;" Latin *deitatem* (nominative *deitas*) "divine nature," Proto-European **deiwos* "god," from root **dyeu-* "to shine," from 1580s as "a being to whom a divine or godlike nature is attributed."

DAEMON (n.)
A transliteration of Greek daimon "lesser god, guiding spirit, tutelary deity." A person who is part mortal and part god.

EUDAEMONIC (adj.)
Producing happiness and well-being, from Greek *eudaimonikos* "conducive to happiness," from *eu* "good" + *daimōn* "guardian, genius."

KING (n.)
A late Old English contraction of *cyning* "king, ruler" from Proto-Germanic **kuningaz,* possibility related to Old English *cynn "family, race"* making a *king* originally the "leader of the people" perhaps from a related prehistoric Germanic word meaning "noble birth" (or "the descendant of a divine race.") Meaning "one who has superiority in a certain field or class" is from 14c.

SOVEREIGN: (n.)
Greatest in status or authority or power, ruler or head of state usually by hereditary right, late 13c. "Superior, ruler, master."

SOVEREIGNTY (n.)
Royal authority; the dominion of a monarch, free from external control, the authority of a state to govern another state. Mid-14c., from Anglo-French *sovereynete*, Old French *souverainete*, from *soverain* meaning "authority, rule, supremacy of power or rank."

SPIRIT (n.)
A vital principle or animating force within living things, a fundamental emotional and activating principle determining one's character, an inclination or tendency of a certain kind, the intended meaning of communication. From late 14c. As "divine substance, divine nature; "the Holy Ghost; divine power," also, extension of divine power to man; "inspiration, a charismatic state; charismatic power, especially of prophecy." Latin *spiritus* "a breathing, breathe, breath of god," hence inspiration; breathe of life," hence "life," also "disposition, character."

CHAPTER TWO: THE ROD

TRUE: (adj.)
Make level, square, balanced, or concentric, accurately fitted, accurately placed, having a legally established claim, consistent with fact or reality, determined with reference to earth's axis rather than the magnetic poles, in tune, accurate in pitch, worthy of being depended on.

Old English *triewe* (West Saxon), *treowe* (Mercian) "faithful, trustworthy, honest, steady." From Proto- Germanic **treuwaz* "having or characterized by good faith" from Proto-Indo-European root **deru-* "be firm, solid, steadfast." Also comfortable to a certain standard (as true north) is from c.1550. Of artifacts, "accurately fitted or shaped" late 15c. Later the notion of "sure, unerring."

WILL (v.1)
Old English *willan, wyllan* "to wish, desire; be willing, be used to; be about to" Gothic *wiljan* "to will, wish, desire," Gothic *waljan* "to choose." The Germanic words are from Proto-European root **wel-(2)* "to wish, will" Sanskrit *vroti* "chooses, prefers" *varyah* "to be chosen, eligible." Old Church Slavic veleti "to command," compare also to Old English *wel* "well" literally "according to one's wish" *wela* "well-being, riches."

LAW (n.)
Old English *lagu* "ordinance, rule prescribed by authority, regulation," also sometimes "right, legal privilege," from Old Norse **lagu* "law," collective plural of *lag* "layer, measure," literally something laid down, "that which is fixed or set." Proto-Indo-European root **legh -* "to lay down, to set or establish."

LAWFUL (adj.)
According to custom or rule or natural law, having a legally established claim. 1300, *laghful*, "rightful, supported by law."

LEGAL (adj.)
Established by or founded upon law or official rules, of or relating to jurisprudence, having legal efficacy or force. mid -15c. "Of or pertaining to the law," from Old French *légal* "legal" pertaining to law," from *lex* "an enactment, a precept, regulation, principle, rule. Related to legere "to gather," from Proto-Indo-European root **leg-* " to collect, gather."

LIBIDO (n.)
In psychoanalysis a term for desire, "Psychic drive or energy, usually associated with sexual instinct," from Latin *libido, lubido* "desire, lust," from *libere* "to be pleasing, to please," from Proto-Indo-European root *leubh-* "to care, desire, love."

VITALITY (n.)
An energetic style, the property of being able to survive and grow, a healthy capacity for vigorous activity. 1590s, from Latin *vitalitatem* (nominative *vitalitas*) "vital force, life" from *vitalis* "pertaining to life."

PURPOSE (n.)
What something is used for, reach a decision, the quality of being determined to do or achieve something; firmness of purpose. C. 1300, "intention, aim, goal," from *proposer* "to put forth," from por- "forth" + Old French *poser* "to put, place" on purpose "by design."

CHAPTER THREE: THE CUP:

RECEIVE (v.)
C. 1300 from Old North French receive (Old French *recoivre*) "seize, take hold of, pick up; welcome, accept," from Latin *recipere* "regain, take back, bring back, carry back, recover; take to oneself, take in, admit."

REFLECT (v.)
LATE 14c., "turn or bend back," early 15c., "divert, to turn aside, deflect," from Old French *reflecter* (14 c.) from Latin *reflectere* "bend back, turn back."

MEDITATE (v.)
1580s, "to ponder, think abstractly, engage in mental contemplation." From Latin *meditatus*. Past participle of *meditari* "to meditate, think over, reflect, consider," form of Proto-European root *med-* "take appropriate measures." From 1590s as "to plan in the mind."

MYSTERY (n.1)
From the Greek mystērion "secret rite or doctrine" (known and practiced by certain initiated persons only) consisting of purifications, sacrificial

offerings, processions, songs, etc. *mystēs* "one who has been initiated." Early 14c., mystery, in a theological sense, "religious truth via divine revelation, hidden spiritual significance, mystical truth."

CHAPTER FOUR: THE SWORD:

PERPENDICULAR (adj.)
Late 15c. *Perpendicular*, of a line, "lying at right angles to the horizon" (in astronomy, navigation, ect.) from Old French *perpendiculer*, from Late Latin *perpendicularis* "vertical, as a plumb line."

HORIZONTAL (adj.)
1500s, "relating to or near the horizon," from French horizontal, from Latin *horizontem*, meaning "flat" (i.e. "parallel to the horizon").

REASON (n.)
C. 1200 "intellectual faculty that adopts actions to ends," also "statement in an argument, statement of explanation or justification," from Anglo-French *raison* "course, matter," Latin *rationem* (nominative *ratio*) "reckoning, understanding, motive, cause," from Proto-European root *re- "to reason, count."

RITE (n.)
Any customary observance or practice, established ceremony, prescribed by a religion. Early 14 c., from Latin *ritus* "religious observance or ceremony, custom, usage," perhaps from Proto-European root *re- "to reason or count."

RIGHT (adj.1)
Old English *riht* "just, good, fair, proper, fitting, straight, direct, erect," "also "rule of conduct, law of the land." Old English *rihtan* "to straighten, rule, set up, set right, amend, guide, govern; restore, replace," Old Norse *retta* "to straighten."

RITUAL (adj.)
Latin *ritualis* "relating to religious *rits*," from *ritus* "religious observance ceremony, custom, from Proto-Indo-European *re-"to reason, count."

RULER (n.)
"One who rules," late 14c. A person who rules or commands.
Ruler (N) measuring stick consisting of a strip of wood with a straight edge that is used for drawing straight lines and measuring lengths.

RULE (n.)
C. 1200 "Principle or maxim governing conduct, formula to which conduct must be conformed" Old French *riule*, Norman reule "rule, custom, (religious) order," from Latin *regula* "straight stick, bar, ruler," figuratively a pattern, a model with derivatives meaning "to direct in a straight line," thus "to lead, rule."

RULING (n.)
Exercising power or authority.

MARK (N.1)
"Trace, impression," Old English mearc (West Saxon), merc(Mercian) "boundary, sign," Dutch *merk* "mark, brand" German Mark "boundary, boundary land" from Proto-European root merg- "boundary, border."

LINE (n.)
A mark that is long relative to its width, the tracing of a moving point, a course of reasoning aimed at demonstrating a truth or falsehood; the methodical process of logical reasoning, a connected series of events or actions or developments, be in line with; form a line along, make a mark or lines on a surface. Latin *linea* "string, plumb-line," also "a mark, bound, limit, goal, line of descent."

CONSTRUCT (v)
1660s, "put together the parts of in their proper place and order," from Latin *constructus*, past participle of *construere* "pile up together, accumulate, build, make, erect."

INSCRIBE (v.)
1550s "to write on or in" (something durable and conspicuous), from Latin *inscribere* "to write on or in" (something) *scrobere* "to write" (from Proto-European root *skribh-* "to cut.) Meaning "to dedicate" (by means of an inscription) is from the 1640s.

DIVISION (n.)
The act or process of dividing, one of the portions into which something is regarded as divided and which together constitute a whole. Late 14c., *divisioun*, "act of separating into parts, portions, or shares, a part separated or distinguished from the rest."

SHARP (adj.)
Old English *scearp* "having a cutting edge, pointed; intellectually acute, active, keen" (of senses) from Proto-European root **sker-* "to cut." The figurative meaning "acute or penetrating in intellect or perception" was in Old English; hence "keenly alive to one's own interest, quick to take advantage."

HONE (n.)
Old English *han* "a stone, rock, (boundary) stone," Old Norse *hein* "hone" from Proto-Indo-European **ko-* "to sharpen, whet." as in "sharpen with a hone, to make perfect and complete.

HONOR (n.)
Worthy of being depended on, not deceptive, marked by truth. 1300, "respectable, virtuous, honorable; deserving honor."

KNOWLEDGE (n.)
The psychological result of perception and learning and reasoning. From Old English *cnawan* know, "perceive a thing to be identical with another, to distinguish, perceive or understand as a fact or truth; know how to do something." Proto-Indo-European root *gno- "to know," *cnawlece*, "acknowledgment of a superior, honor, worship."

SWORD (n.)
Old English *sweord*, Northumbrian "*sword*" from Proto-Germanic **swerdam, swertha-* literally "the cutting weapon," from Proto-Indo European roo*t *swer-* "to cut, pierce."

UPRIGHT (adj.)
In vertical position, not sloping, upright position, or posture, of moral excellence, a vertical structural member as a post or stake. Old English *upriht* "erect, face-upward," German aufrecht, (Old Norse uprettr) Figurative sense of "good, honest, adhering to rectitude."

CHAPTER FIVE: THE PANTACLE:

MATTER (n.)
That which has mass and occupies space, having weight, having consequence, some situation or event that is thought about. C. 1200 materie, "the subject of a mental act or a course of thought, speech, or expression," Old French *matere* "subject, content, character," Latin materia "substance from which something is made."

SACRED (adi.)
Devoted exclusively to a single purpose. Made or declared to be holy; devoted to a deity or some religious ceremony or use, made worthy of respect or dedication. Proto-European, *shnk* - "to make sacred," finds cognates in Hittite *saklai* "costumes, rites." Latin *saceres*, from Proto-European *sak*- "to sanctity." The Latin nasalized form is *sancire* "make sacred, confirm, ratify, ordain."

SACRAMENT (n.)
Olds French *sacrament* "consecration; mystery," from Latin *sacramentum*, "a solemn oath" late Old English, "an outward and visible sign of inward and spiritual grace." The meaning "arcane knowledge; a secret; a mystery; a divine mystery," in English is from late 14c. "A solemn oath, pledge, covenant; a ceremony accompanying the taking of an oath or the making of a pledge."

COMMUNION (n.)
Latin ecclesiastical language for "participation in the sacrament," Derived from *com*- "with, together" + "oneness, union." In English from mid 15c. As "the sacrament of the Eucharist," Late 14c., "participation in something; doctrine, discipline" from the 1610s as "intercourse between two or more."

CAUSE (n.)
C.1200, "reason or motive for a decision, grounds for action; motive," from Old French *cause* "cause, reason; lawsuit, case in law"

EFFECT (n.)
Mid-14c., "execution or completion," (of an act) from Old French *efet* (13c., Modern French *effet*) "result, execution, completion, ending," from

Latin *effectus* "accomplishment, performance." From late 14c. As "power or capacity to produce an intended result; efficacy, effectiveness," also "that which follows from something else; a consequence or result." From early 15c as "intended result, purpose, object, intent."

ECONOMIC (adj.)
Concerned with worldly necessities of life, using the minimum of time or resources necessary for effectiveness. 1590s, "pertaining to management of a household," from Latin *oeconomicus* "of domestic economy." Greek *oikonomikos* "practice in the management of a household or family."

CRAFT (n.)
Old English *cræft* (West Saxon, Northumbrian), *-creft* (Kentish) "power, physical strength, might," from Proto-Germanic **krab-/*kraf*, German *Kraft* "strength, skill," Old Norse *kraptr* "strength, virtue")

CRAFTY (adj.)
Mid-12c., *crafti*, "skillful, clever, learned," from Old English *cræftig* "strong, powerful,"

COMPOSITION (n.)
A mixture of ingredients, the way in which someone or something is composed, something that is created by arranging several things to form a unified whole. Late 14c, *composicioun*, "action of combing," also "manner in which a thing is composed," Latin *compositionem* "a putting together, connecting, arranging, componere; to put together, to collect a whole from several parts," from *com* "with, together" +*ponere* "to place."

SYNCHRONICITY (n.)
1953 from synchronic +ity . Originally in Jung. The relation that exists when things occur at the same time.

Booklist:

The many components that make up this book can also be explored further here:

The Temple of Man, R.A. Schwaller de Lubiz
Essential Jung, Carl Jung
Love and Will, Rollo May
Book 4, Aleister Crowley
Man, State and Economy, Murray N. Rothbard
Divine Craftsmanship, Preliminaries to a Spirituality of Work, Jean Hani
Dictionary of Symbols, J.E. Cirlot
Psychology and the Occult, Carl Jung
The Will to Power, Nietzsche
The Art of War, Sun Tsu
The Act of Will, Roberto Assagioli, M.D.
The Willpower Instinct, Kelly Mcgonigal
Good Strategy/ Bad Strategy, Richard Rumelt
Sources of Power, How people make decisions, Gary Klein
The Mystery of the Grail, Julius Evola
Critique of Pure Reason, Immanuel Kant
Secrets of the Pyramids, Peter Tomkins
Secret Teachings of all Ages, Manly P. Hall
Etymonline English Dictionary

LIVE YOUR WILL @ www.thekingscurriculum.com

www.ingramcontent.com/pod-product-compliance
Lightning Source LLC
Chambersburg PA
CBHW071240070526
44583CB00017B/2266